LANCASTER HOUSE   *London's Greatest Town House*

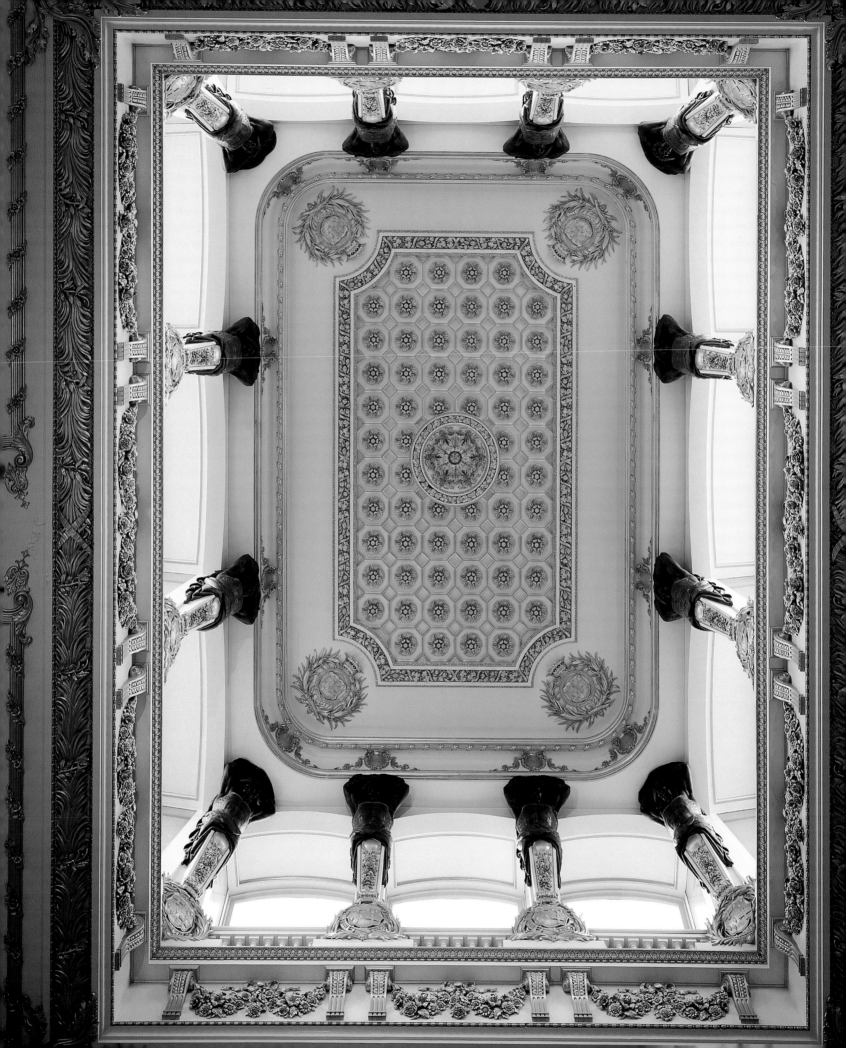

LANCASTER HOUSE

London's Greatest Town House

James Yorke

MERRELL

To Primrose, Philip and Henry

FRONTISPIECE
Lantern of the Principal Staircase,
Lancaster House. The herms were
supplied by the firm of Francis
Bernasconi, London's leading
decorative plasterer. The idea was
probably borrowed from J.H. Mansart's
designs for the Salon of the Château de
Marly, and had been used as early as
1824 in Londonderry House by Philip
Wyatt.

PAGES 6–7
Lancaster House: south front.

First Published 2001 by
Merrell Publishers Limited
42 Southwark Street
London SE1 1UN
WWW.MERRELLPUBLISHERS.COM

Text © 2001
James Yorke
Pictures ©
the copyright holders; for details see page 189

Distributed in the USA *and Canada by*
Rizzoli International Publications, Inc.
through St Martin's Press
175 Fifth Avenue
New York, New York 10010

*British Library Cataloguing-in-Publication
Data*
Lancaster House : London's greatest town
house
1.Lancaster House – History 2.Architecture,
Domestic – England – London – History
I.Title
728´.09421
ISBN 1 85894 126 1

Produced by Merrell Publishers Limited
Edited by Iain Ross
Designed by Paul Barnes, Modern Typography

Set in Brunel and Caslon Egyptian, based on
the world's first sans-serif typeface first
shown in Caslon specimen book of 1815
Brunel designed by Paul Barnes
*Caslon Egyptian digitized for this book by
Modern Typography, 2001*

Contents

Acknowledgements

The publication of this book could not have come about without liberal funding from The Paul Mellon Center for Studies in British Art, the South Square Trust, the Marc Fitch Fund, the Scouloudi Foundation in association with the Institute for Historical Research, the late Miss Isobel Thornley Bequest to the University of London, the Oliver Ford Charitable Trust, Sotheby's and a Stroud Bursary awarded by the Society of Architectural Historians of Great Britain. I am deeply indebted to these foundations for their generosity. I am as much indebted to Professor David Watkin and Giles Waterfield for their unstinting support in my various applications.

In writing a book of this nature, one inevitably imposes on the kindness, hospitality, expertise and goodwill of many colleagues, friends, owners and custodians of family papers. I should like to express my particular thanks to my PhD supervisor, Professor J. Mordaunt Crook, for his constant encouragement, inspiration and much-needed constructive criticism. I should also like to express undying gratitude to Dudley Fowkes and the staff of the Staffordshire County Record Office for their constant helpfulness, humour and good-natured compliance with endless demands over the last decade. I should also like to thank Elizabeth, Countess of Sutherland, the late Duke of Rutland, and Dorothy and Philip Staverley, the duke's secretary and archivist, for their kindness and hospitality in allowing me to see unpublished manuscripts in their possession, which yielded much priceless information. I am also indebted to my colleagues, past and present, at the Victoria and Albert Museum, London: Frances Collard, Howard Coutts, Philippa Glanville, John Hardy, Kenneth Jackson, Simon Jervis, Dr Norbert Jopek, Sarah Medlam, Dr Tessa Murdoch, Amanda Robertson, Dr Carolyn Sarjentson, Dr Deborah Swallow, Peter Thornton, Moira Thunder, the late Dr Clive Wainwright and Christopher Wilk. I could not have lasted the course without the constant encouragement and support of my wife, Primrose; in addition, her proof-reading has saved me from countless howlers.

I should also like to thank the following friends and colleagues for generously sharing their expertise with me and courteously complying with various requests: Dr David Blisset, Dr Antonia Boström, John Charlton, Lord Crathorne, Joe Friedman, Helen Guiterman, John Harris, Niall Hobhouse, Florian Illes, Dr John Martin Robinson, Charles Sebag Montefiore, Robert Stanley Morgan and Richard Wisker.

Thanks are also owed to the following: James Collet-White, Bedfordshire County Record Office; Dr Charles Ridway, Castle Howard Archives, Yorkshire; Christian Baulez, Château de Versailles, France; Jeremy Rex Parkes, Christie's Archives, London; Philip Ward-Jackson, Conway Library, Courtauld Institute of Art, London; Barbara Peters, Coutts Archives, London; Michael Tree, The Crown Estate, London; Jennifer Gill, Durham County Record Office; Dr Michael Turner, English Heritage, London; Ken Clare and Philip Kiberd, Foreign and Commonwealth Office Records and Historical Department, London; Angela Pellat and Victoria Lane, Goldsmiths' Hall, London; Dr Mary Beale and David Law, Government Collection of Works of Art, London; Bryan Burrough and Sylvia Jones, Government Hospitality, London; Lucy Wood, Lady Lever Art Gallery, Merseyside; Jacqui Booker, Dorothy Phillips and Phillys Rogers, Lancaster House, London; Bill Rieder, The Metropolitan Museum of Art, New York; Sally Brooks, Dr Celina Fox and Eva Yocum, Museum of London; Christopher Brown, Clare Bunkham and Gabrielle Finaldi, The National Gallery, London; Tim Clifford, The National Gallery of Scotland, Edinburgh; Robin Sanderson, The Natural History Museum, London; Dr Steven Parissien, The Paul Mellon Centre for Studies in British Art, London; Melanie Aspey, The Rothschild Archive, London; Pamela Clarke, Royal Archives, Windsor Castle; Hugh Roberts and Jonathan Marsden, The Royal Collection, London; Ian Gow, Royal Commission on the Ancient and Historical Monuments of Scotland, Edinburgh; Professor Sir Howard Colvin, St John's College, Oxford; James Miller and Mario Tavella, Sotheby's, London; and John Greenacombe, Survey of London.

Introduction

York House (1825–27); Stafford House (1827–1914); Lancaster House (since 1914): three names for one house – but what a house. Situated at the bottom of Green Park and facing St James's Park stands London's greatest town house. The term 'town house' may seem a typically English understatement; and yet, if more of these buildings were still standing, they would surely be compared with the *palazzi* of any great Italian city. The latter were built for the leading families by the finest architects of their day, and so were the London town houses. To someone as well-travelled and cosmopolitan as Benjamin Disraeli, Lancaster House had all the glamour of a palace in Vicenza, the Italian city that most bears the mark of Andrea Palladio. Even Queen Victoria was to say to Harriet, Duchess of Sutherland, "I come from my house to your palace".[1]

But what exactly was a town house? Put simply, it was the power base of a noble family in the capital city, much as the country house was in the provinces. The town house took the form of a large and often free-standing residence, and was usually named after the title bestowed upon that family. Among other things, London was the centre of social life, and the grander a family's residence, the greater its prestige. Lancaster House may have been the greatest town house, but its foundations were laid in 1825, almost the last time when such a building would have been possible. In the preceding centuries, when areas around St James's or Oxford Street were virtually fields, a noble could build himself a large house on the edges of – and thus incorporate it into – a fashionable part of town. However, the relentless expansion of London during the latter half of the nineteenth century, and the ever-decreasing amount of land available in the desirable parts, meant that huge houses of the order of Montagu or Dorchester House were hardly feasible after about 1860.

Plate 1
Ivy and bulrush ornament (detail), supplied by George Jackson & Son for the former South-West Drawing Room (also known as the Green Velvet Room), Lancaster House. Benjamin Wyatt singled out for praise "the beautiful execution of the Ivy ornament" in the room.

The twentieth century has shown little mercy towards the town house: all too often regarded as anachronisms that stood on sites more valuable than the buildings themselves, they were relentlessly demolished from the 1920s onwards, and to precious few murmurs of protest. However, nostalgia for what was never known can be a surprisingly potent force: in 1981 public awareness of the town house was rekindled to no small extent by the televising of Evelyn Waugh's novel *Brideshead Revisited*. Many who followed the television series were made aware for the first time of such buildings as Marchmain House (filmed inside Bridgewater House), and of the fact that beautiful people like Lord Sebastian Flyte and Lady Julia Mottram really grew up there, as well as at Brideshead. The purpose of this book is to paint a portrait of the greatest example of such houses. Those who lived and grew up at Lancaster (then known as Stafford) House were not necessarily as glamorous as Waugh's fictional characters, but they did actually exist, and they often played out dramas in real life as bizarre as any novel: they breathed spirit into that large Bath-stone-clad building in St James's.

But what form should this portrait take? At its most basic level, every house has to be built, it has to work, and it has to have some recognizable use. If it was owned by a family as rich as the Sutherlands, it is bound to have contained some worthwhile paintings or *objets d'art*. If it is no longer occupied by that family, then there must be some reason. These questions this book will attempt to answer.

The process of building was often a fraught affair. The beginning could not have been more inauspicious: for the 'Grand Old' Duke of York, beset with insuperable debts, to embark on such an enterprise could be described only as foolhardy, but then he was besotted with a duchess addicted to schemes that verged on the megalomaniac. Luckily, the 2nd Marquis of Stafford was prepared to take it over, and his eldest son to bring the works to a splendid conclusion, despite the fact that the latter had three architects working – often against each other – at the same time. Once the house was completed, its interiors were noted for their lavish decoration in the manner of Louis XIV, the earliest form of Rococo revival. Lancaster House was also regarded as a palace of art, mainly associated with Spanish masterpieces, especially two outstanding Murillos. But children were also brought up in these surroundings; nearly fifty household servants went about their daily duties; and countless balls, receptions and committee meetings were held there. All manner of nineteenth- and early twentieth-century celebrities came, ranging from Harriet Beecher Stowe, General Garibaldi and Frédéric Chopin to Dame Nellie Melba and the young Winston Churchill. Such opulence and splendour could not last for ever. Stafford House, the town house of the nineteenth century, became Lancaster House or the London Museum, London's answer to Paris's Musée Carnavalet, between the wars. This was at a time when civic museums were fashionable, but the political climate militated against the town house. (Acrimonious family quarrels also played their part.) Since the Second World War, Britain has lost her empire, but still needs a symbolic building to create the right impression overseas. The ceaseless demand for international conferences and the museum's need for larger premises have meant that the London Museum has moved out and finally settled by London Wall, under the name of the Museum of London, while the Foreign Office has taken over Lancaster House.

It is as if a house as great as Lancaster House could not be content with just one name. York House, Stafford House and Lancaster House are one and the same building. The story demands that the house should be referred to by one of its three different names at different stages of the narrative – and mostly as Stafford House. It would clearly be as inappropriate to say that the Duke of York was determined to build himself 'Lancaster House' as it would be to say that Zimbabwe's future was settled at the 'Stafford House Conference'. Another complicating factor is the use of titles: courtesy titles, belonging to the son and heir, differ from those that go with peerage, and they in turn usually change in the rare event of an elevation to higher rank. Therefore the same person may have as many as three different names or titles: Earl Gower, on succeeding his father, became 2nd Marquis of Stafford and ended up as 1st Duke of Sutherland. Both the 1st and 2nd duke had exactly the same Christian name: to call them both 'George Granville' would only confuse, but, unlike their successors, they had no universally recognized nicknames. With the 3rd and 4th dukes, we are more fortunate: the former was widely known as 'Staff' (short for his courtesy title, Marquis of Stafford) and the latter as 'Strath' (short for his, Earl of Strathnaver), and, when appropriate, they will be referred to as such. With these factors in mind, the reader is invited to enter a world of private palaces, best exemplified by that three-in-one, York House, Stafford House and Lancaster House.

1 *From York House to Stafford House*

In 1825 London was the capital of the richest and most powerful nation in the world. And yet, despite its unrivalled size, it seemed paltry and almost provincial when compared with Paris or St Petersburg. Nevertheless, following the victory at Waterloo, there were those anxious to 'improve' London: most famous was John Nash, who, as Architect to the King's Works, served as the Prince Regent's instrument in his quest to "eclipse Napoleon". But, as a public servant, Nash had to reconcile his employer's wishes with the constraints of the Treasury. Not so a certain Colonel Frederick William Trench (1775–1859; *pl. 3*), veteran of the Walcheren expedition of 1809, Tory Member of Parliament for the town of Cambridge and author of *Collection of Papers relating to the Thames Quay, with Hints for some further improvements in the metropolis* (London 1827). Unofficially attached to the Duke of Rutland's household as an *arbiter elegantiae* since about 1817, Colonel Trench had secured the desired entrée into High Tory and royal circles. To the Duchess of Rutland he was "Frederick le Grand", but to his enemies "Toady Trench" or "the Irish impostor". Trench's intended "further improvements" had a mixture of dash and lunacy, but they were well received in royal circles, as was his scheme to create a new embankment from Westminster to London Bridge. However, opposition from the Thames wharfers and tradesmen with shops along the Strand, coupled with the deaths of both his leading patrons, the Duchess of Rutland in 1825 and the Duke of York in 1827, eventually forced him to abandon the idea.

The greatest of Trench's precious few plans to get beyond the drawing board was York House. Now known as Lancaster House, this monumental edifice was originally intended as the London palace of the heir apparent, Prince Frederick Augustus, the 'Grand Old' Duke of York (1763–1827; *pl. 4*). As second son of George III, the Duke of York held the post of Commander-in-Chief of the British Army for most of the Napoleonic Wars, and maintained a reputation for

Plate 2
Lantern of Picture Gallery, Lancaster House, with *St Chrysogonus Being Borne by Angels* by GUERCINO (1590–1666). The painting was probably brought to England from the church of San Crisogono in Rome by Alexander Day in 1801 and was moved from Bridgewater House to Stafford House by December 1834. Note the date-palm decoration in the piers, designed by Charles Barry in 1838, and one of the main causes of Benjamin Wyatt's resignation as architect of the State Apartments. The windows were originally decorated with embossed glass by John Henning, Jr (1801–1857).

competent administration. Nevertheless, he is unheroically remembered for his "ten thousand men" and his scandalous liaison – which forced him to resign – with Mary Anne Clarke, whom a number of army officers had bribed to suggest to the duke that they might be promoted. By about July 1824, if not earlier, it was widely known in society that the Duke of York and Elizabeth, Duchess of Rutland (*pl. 5*) were lovers. Indeed, the two pointedly sat next to each other, in the presence of her husband, on a barge that Colonel Trench had borrowed from the Company of Merchant Taylors for a meeting at which he could unfurl his plans for the proposed Thames Quay. A year later Harriet Arbuthnot, friend and confidante of the Duke of Wellington, was to write disapprovingly: "they are like a boy & girl of 17 & 15 &, when one recollects that the one is 62 & the other an old grandmother, it really is disgusting."[1] (In all fairness, the duchess was only forty-three when she became a grandmother: her eldest daughter, Lady Elizabeth Frederica, had married in 1821 and produced a son in 1823.)

Elizabeth, Duchess of Rutland (1780–1825) was daughter of the 4th Earl of Carlisle, and spent her childhood at Castle Howard: growing up in such a grand house may well have given her a taste for building on a megalomaniac scale. In 1799 she married John Henry, 5th Duke of Rutland, who two years later employed James Wyatt (1746–1813), Surveyor General to the King's Works, to transform his seat at Belvoir Castle, Leicestershire, from a plain classical house into a Gothic castle. James Wyatt died in a coach accident in 1813, but a disastrous fire in November 1816 provided the duchess with the impetus to rebuild much of the castle in an even more uncompromisingly Gothic style, to the designs of Sir John Thoroton, a cousin of the duke and family chaplain. However, the duchess's tastes were not confined to Gothic: Belvoir Castle included an classical dining room and later a drawing room, known as the Elizabeth Saloon, decorated in the French style. A visit to Paris in 1814 had given the duchess a love for all things connected with the *ancien régime*, which seemed to be returning with the restoration of the French monarchy under Louis XVIII. Some ten years later, the chance availability of some early Rococo boiserie, thought to have come from a château originally belonging to Mme de Maintenon, morganatic wife of Louis XIV, gave her the wherewithal to create the Elizabeth Saloon at Belvoir Castle, and with it a fashion for the Louis XIV style. This was the style she thought most suitable for the interiors of the Duke of York's new house, to be built on the site of his existing residence, Godolphin House (*pl. 6*), situated at the south-east corner of Green Park.

By 1825 the two architects most in favour with the Duchess of Rutland were Benjamin (1775–1855) and Philip Wyatt (died 1835), sons of James Wyatt. After an unsuccessful spell working for the East India Company in Calcutta, Benjamin Dean (*pl. 7*), the eldest, returned to England in 1802. In 1807 he became secretary

Plate 3
UNKNOWN ARTIST, *Sir Frederick William Trench*, c. 1827, oil on canvas, London, National Portrait Gallery. Trench is posing with plans for his Thames Quay 'improvements'.

Plate 4
UNKNOWN ARTIST after JOHN JACKSON (1778–1831), *Frederick Augustus, Duke of York and Albany*, 1822, oil on canvas, London, National Portrait Gallery. Former Commander-in-Chief of the British Army and heir apparent to the throne between 1820 and 1827, the year he died, the 'Grand Old Duke' never lived to move into York House, the building of which greatly added to his already prodigious debts.

Plate 5

GEORGE SANDERS (*fl. 1810–1820*),
*Elizabeth, Duchess of Rutland (b. 1780,
m. 1799, d. 1825), c. 1816*, oil on canvas,
Belvoir Castle, Leicestershire.
Passionate about building, architecture
and her husband's estates, Duchess
Elizabeth was described by a
contemporary, Harriet Arbuthnot, as
having "all the follies & weaknesses of
a beautiful woman, but ... a masculine
strength of mind, an elevated taste ...".

to Sir Arthur Wellesley, later Duke of Wellington, and in 1809 decided to follow in
his father's footsteps and become an architect. His early triumph had been the
Theatre Royal, Drury Lane (1811–12) and he had devised unexecuted schemes for
a vast Waterloo Palace (1815–16). His first encounter with the Duchess of Rutland –
not necessarily in the most ideal circumstances – was probably when he came to
Belvoir Castle in 1813 to collect outstanding amounts owed to his late father.[2] His
younger brother Philip had been groomed to take over his father's practice, and
had been actively engaged in making designs for Colonel Trench's Thames Quay.
Philip was affable and inspired – indeed William Beckford, who had employed
their father at Fonthill Abbey, called him "Sweetness". Unfortunately, he lacked
the discipline of his often difficult and ill-tempered older brother, known to
Beckford as "Bitterness".[3]

When the Duke of York first acquired Godolphin House in 1807, he intended to
add two drawing rooms at the west end,[4] but nothing came of it. By 1811 the house
had become little more than an asset on which to raise a mortgage of £30,000
from Messrs Cox, Greenwood & Hammersley, bankers to the army.[5] Not even his
new status from 1820 as heir apparent to the throne induced him to begin works.
Only in July 1823 did the duke seek permission from the Lords of the Treasury to
proceed.[6] He was almost certainly prompted by Colonel Trench and the Duchess
of Rutland, who had first discussed such possibilities at the beginning of the year.[7]
By August 1824 he had secured a loan of £10,000 from Nathan Rothschild,

Plate 8
W. Daniell (1769–1837), *Sir Robert Smirke*, 1808, from an engraving after George Dance, London, National Portrait Gallery. Smirke was the first architect of York House but he was supplanted after about three months' work in 1825. Knighted in 1832, Smirke returned as architect in charge in 1833 and remained thus until 1838, when ill health forced him to retire.

Plate 9
Robert Smirke (1780–1867), *Designs for York House, c. 1825*, ink on paper, London, Westminster City Archives. These were on a far more modest scale than the Duchess of Rutland envisaged for her lover, the Duke of York.

presumably for such a purpose.[8] But it was in March 1825 that the Duke of York came into conflict with the king over his new house. As Mrs Arbuthnot wrote, he was "rather in disgrace with the King … he positively refused to give permission to the D. of York to build a new house on the site of his old one. The Duke of York, however, says he can do it without his leave and he protests that he will, which I suppose will widen the breach between them."[9]

Surprisingly enough, the commission was first awarded not to the Wyatt brothers but to Robert Smirke (*pl. 8*), an architect attached to the Office of Works at about that time – his activities can be dated with certainty only from April 1825.[10] The king disapproved of Smirke's plans, but was to show far greater enthusiasm for those of Benjamin and Philip Wyatt. In a letter to the *Morning Chronicle* (26 April 1826) the duke wrote: "after the first plans [*i.e.* those of Smirke] were made, they were submitted to those whom I was bound to consult [*i.e.* the king and the Duchess of Rutland], and strongly objected to by them; alterations were then called for which were equally disapproved."

Robert Smirke's first spell at York House lasted only two months. Just as he was about to be dismissed, *The Times* (26 May 1825) was able to report that demolition was almost complete. Smirke's surviving designs of the period include two undated lithographs (*pl. 9*),[11] one of a modest building with attic towers, balustrading and an arcaded *piano nobile* but no orders; and the other dominated by a hexastyle Ionic portico, the upper storey articulated with Corinthian pilasters.[12] Smirke's elevations of the grand staircase (1825), with an arcade supported by Corinthian pilasters (*pl. 10*) were probably an attempt to produce something in the Wyatt idiom, and thus retain the commission.[13] After all, the king had been sufficiently fired by Wyatt's plans to "command" the Duke of York to adopt them.[14] The Duchess of Rutland almost certainly orchestrated the replacement of Smirke, but her precise actions remain uncertain: after the Duke of York's death, his private secretary, Sir Herbert Taylor, destroyed all their letters.[15]

In June 1825 Smirke was ignominiously replaced by Benjamin and Philip Wyatt. In retaliation, he had Benjamin censured the following year by the Architect's Society for breaking Regulation No. 12, which prohibited any member from soliciting or undertaking the commission of another without prior consultation. Wyatt responded not only by resigning but also by publishing his defence and the above-mentioned letter from the Duke of York in the *Morning Chronicle*. He alleged that Smirke had done the same thing over the new Post Office and the British Museum. Some eight years later, Wyatt would pay the price for his bravado, as we shall see below.

Oblivious to Robert Smirke's sensibilities, the Duchess of Rutland laid the foundation stone of York House on 17 July 1825,[16] and proceeded to direct the

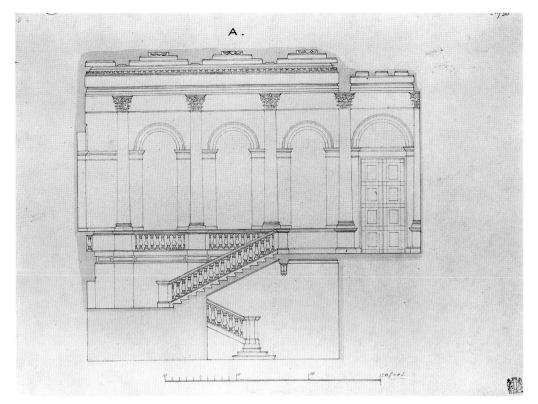

A.

building until her sudden death on 25 November that year. By the end of August the adjoining Queen's Library, the work of William Kent, had been pulled down,[17] and by 18 September the building had reached ground level: the vaulting in the cellar was complete, and Bramah's ironwork for supporting the Principal Staircase was being installed.[18] Wyatt entertained the idea – never to be executed – of crowning the building with pediments decorated with military trophies or groups of allegorical figures. He also referred to his brother Philip and himself working on "clear drawings" of the new building for both the Duchess of Rutland and the king (*pls. 11, 37*).[19] Not all of Wyatt's ideas met with the Duchess's approval: she was unhappy with the excessive projection of the North Portico (*pl. 12*) and the tone of the *verde antico* scagliola columns. On the first point, Wyatt pleaded the need to accommodate carriages, and on the second, he assured her that lighter-green versions could be made, although the light from the lantern and gilding of the capitals would very much brighten the overall effect. By the end of November the ground floor was complete, and earlier that month the Duke of York had laid on a banquet of beef and beer for the builders, to celebrate the progress of the work.[20]

The death of the Duchess of Rutland from a burst appendix left both her husband and the Duke of York desolate, but (surprisingly) with no hard feelings towards each other. As Lady Williams Wynn wrote six weeks later: "the

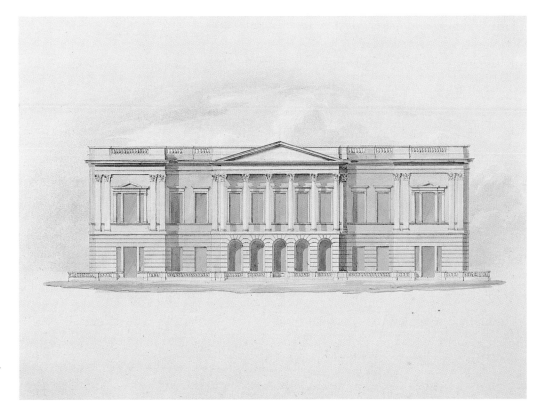

Plate 11
BENJAMIN (1775–1855) and
PHILIP (died 1835) WYATT, *Elevation of
the South Front of York House*, 1825,
watercolour, The Royal Collection.

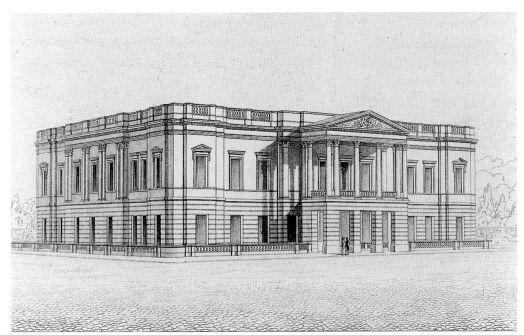

Plate 12
J. LE KEUX (1787–1868), *York House:
Elevation of the North and East Fronts*,
1827, from an engraving after designs
by Benjamin and Philip Wyatt, from
F.W. TRENCH, *Thames Quay, with
Hints for some further improvements in
the metropolis*. Elizabeth, Duchess of
Rutland criticized Benjamin Wyatt for
making the portico project too much.

disconsolate Duke of York has been passing a fortnight with the disconsolate Widower, mingling ... their sighs and regrets over the Ecarte table, and with their united tears making a pool in the middle."[21] The duchess had provided the galvanizing force that enabled the new building to rise up with remarkable speed, having reached roof level by the new year, as the 21 January 1826 edition of the *Literary Gazette* reported. Thanks to her and indeed her two architects, the article could refer to "four perfect fronts", a rusticated ground floor, and the more princely appearance of a house with only two storeys and an upper floor concealed by balustrading. The addition of broad terraces to the south and west fronts was hailed as "quite a new feature in the architecture of the metropolis". As for the interiors, the hall would be lit by a "superb lantern", the ground floor would be taken up with the duke's apartments, and the principal floor with state rooms, a dining room and a gallery some 130 feet long.

Even without her guiding presence, building continued apace. *The Times* (5 June 1826) reported that the exterior of the house was largely completed within eleven months of the foundation stone being laid, a fact verified by a watercolour by T.H. Shepherd, dated *c.* 1826 (*pl. 13*). By November 1826 the Duke of York, although in the last stages of dropsy of the stomach, was thinking of moving in as soon as possible.[22] By then the ground floor was habitable,[23] and even if the duke never recovered sufficiently to settle in his new palace, a few of his servants did. Among them was his coachman, a Mr Fenn, whose unceremonious eviction would be reported in *The Times* (23 December 1828) two years later. However, while the Duke of York was still alive, the house remained largely a shell: Richard Todd supplanted Samuel Taylor of Rochester, Smirke's brother-in-law, as supplier of bricks, and Philip Nowell clad the building with Bath stone.[24] On the inside, William Croggon, the scagliola specialist, provided *verde antico* columns for the landing of the Principal Staircase and *giallo antico* ones for the vestibule. However, he had to content himself with selling off the finished items at half-price to the Marquis of Stafford when the building eventually changed hands.[25] The ornamental plasterwork was in the hands of Francis Bernasconi & Co., and this included "eight colossal caryatids" on site,[26] destined for the lantern of the Principal Staircase. When C.R. Cockerell paid a visit on 15 December 1826, enough work had been completed inside to leave him in no doubt as to the style intended for the interiors – "the worst of Louis 14th".[27]

About £65,155 had been paid out on the building by the time the Duke of York died on 7 January 1827.[28] In addition to Rothschild's loan, the duke spent a total of £18,950 from his current account at Messrs Coutts & Co,[29] and during the last six months of his life he was advanced £47,000 by the Commissioners of Woods, Forests and Land Revenues.[30] This sum was made up of £22,000, mostly raised

Plate 16
SIR THOMAS LAWRENCE (1769–1830),
Earl Gower [later 2nd Duke of
Sutherland], *c.* 1828, oil on canvas,
Sutherland, Dunrobin Castle,
Sutherland Trust. This painting would
have been painted soon after Earl
Gower's father had taken possession of
what was now called Stafford House.

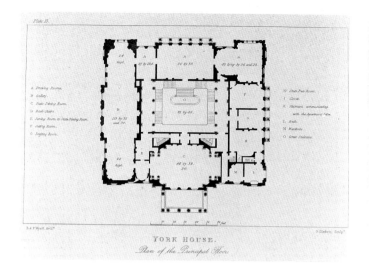

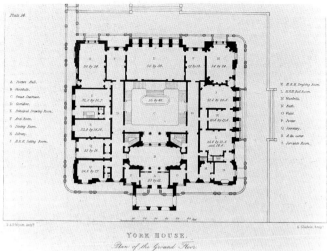

YORK HOUSE.
Plan of the Principal Floor

YORK HOUSE.
Plan of the Ground Floor

With his purchase money accruing interest in exchequer bonds at Coutts Bank, Stafford took possession of York House on 14 February 1828, renaming it Stafford House,[63] and work could at last begin, with Benjamin Wyatt as architect in charge. The basement, ground floor, attics and west elevation of the Principal Floor were to be completed, but the rest glazed and left as a shell. On 16 February 1828 Wyatt sent Lord Stafford a document headed *Queries to be submitted to the Marquis of Stafford relative to the completion of York House*.[64] He also forwarded "a section of the intended Embellishment of the Lantern and Cove under the Lantern, and the Great Staircase...".[65] At a meeting that month at West Hill, the Staffords' house in Wimbledon, the main plans were decided: the walls of the Principal Staircase were now to be decorated exclusively with scagliola, and those of the other rooms were to be left flat and unadorned with Louis XIV ornaments, so as to provide more space in which to hang Stafford's paintings. Stafford evidently followed his wife's advice to "be on his guard with Wyatt in the details, as he will of course wish to follow the same sort of course in the conclusion that he was led into in the beginning of his work".[66]

The second phase of building lasted from February 1828 until August 1829. Although details were altered, the work went largely to plan, with pressure on Wyatt to finish it as quickly as possible. By September 1828, the Dining Room, Ante-Rooms and Drawing Room were ready for gilding and painting; the bedrooms and attics were ready for upholsterers; and scagliola decoration on the first landing almost complete.[67] As many as eight gilded terms had been placed in the lantern (*frontispiece*), and the foot of the stairs was almost ready to take the pavement and marble. In December Wyatt expressed his dismay at Lord Stafford's decision to have the walls of the dining room painted white: "white will form a most deplorable ground to hang pictures on" (like the notorious yellow

Plate 17
G. GLADWIN (*fl.* 1830s), *York House: Plan of the Principal Floor*, from an engraving after designs by Benjamin and Philip Wyatt, from F.W. TRENCH, *Thames Quay, with Hints for some further improvements in the metropolis,* 1827. Bar alterations on the west wing, Trench's layout was adopted by the Sutherlands and left largely unaltered until they sold the leasehold in 1913.

Plate 18
G. GLADWIN (*fl.* 1830s), *York House: Plan of the Ground Floor*, from an engraving after designs by BENJAMIN and PHILIP WYATT, from F.W. TRENCH, *Thames Quay, with Hints for some further improvements in the metropolis,* 1827.

damask hangings in the Waterloo Gallery of Apsley House).[68] By February 1829
the scagliola was complete bar the final polish,[69] and in April Morel & Seddon's
men were applying silk hangings to the various state rooms on the ground floor.[70]
Although Loch's letters were amicable and congratulatory by the end of this
phase, Lady Stafford was losing her patience: "it was with the greatest driving and
difficulty", she wrote, "we cd obtain getting locks put in & trifles finished in the
private apartments to enable us to place our things there".[71] Even if Lord Stafford
would not hear a word against Wyatt,[72] his wife was less than enthusiastic.

Throughout this phase, Wyatt remained loyal to his tradesmen: Messrs
Bernasconi, Todd, Nowell, Bramah & Croggon resumed where they had left off
at York House. In addition, he used Morant & Son for painting and gilding; the
London Marble Company for decorative moulding and paving; Browne & Co. for
State Apartment chimney pieces; and M. Mazzoni for modelling the massive

Plate 20
View of the former ground-floor
Drawing Room, Lancaster House, with
original curtain pelmets, pier glasses
and pier tables supplied by Morel &
Seddon in 1829. The decoration on the
door is probably the work of a carver by
the name of Daniel Horton, and dates
from 1828.

bearded terms that supported the staircase (*pl. 19*). Much of the rich decoration in the ground-floor State Apartments was executed in wood "to the French Design with Foliage and Shell ornaments" by a Daniel Horton, a specialist carver (*pl. 20*).[73] During this phase of the building, Jackson & Son's composition putty, so copiously used after 1833, was confined to the Principal Staircase cantilevers "with rich moulded fronts & scrolled sides".[74] Bernasconi was responsible for the decorative plasterwork on the coves and cornices of the State Apartments and the lantern of the Principal Staircase (*frontispiece*), and these were gilded and painted by Morant. Both the State Apartments and those of Lord and Lady Stafford were furnished in a mixture of styles, ranging from William Kent Revival in the Dining Room (*pl. 29*) to Louis XIV in the Drawing Room and Ante-Rooms (*pl. 20*), by Morel & Seddon.[75] Indeed, Nicholas Morel, one of the partners of this firm, had recently been sent by the government to Paris to glean the latest French styles for the new decorations of Windsor Castle. As a result, he was sufficiently knowledgeable of all things French to work independently of Wyatt.[76]

During this phase, Wyatt was able to execute his *tour de force*, the Principal Staircase. Croggon's work amounted to just over £7,000,[77] and his lavish decorations are recorded in David Roberts's painting of the Principal Staircase (*pl. 21*), commissioned by the Marquis of Stafford in 1830 and completed by September 1832.[78] These two factors, combined with the relatively modest scagliola bills – mostly of a repairing nature – of Wyatt Parker during the 1840s, refute any idea that the upper-floor decorations were designed by Sir Charles Barry at a later stage. Joseph Bramah's masterpiece (*pl. 104*), the gilt iron balustrading very similar to that of Apsley House, was completed by April 1829, at a cost of just over £700.[79] Lady Stafford's praise of the staircase of Apsley House made Wyatt write nervously to Loch: "I however hope that Lady S is not better pleased with that work than with her own Staircase."[80]

By August 1829 Wyatt must have felt well satisfied at the completion of his work at Stafford House. Like some *deus ex machina*, Lord Stafford had appeared and salvaged what could have been the wreck of Wyatt's most prestigious commission to date. Once Earl Gower became 2nd duke, there was every reason to assume that he would turn to Wyatt to bring the building to a triumphant conclusion. However, this was not to be. Although no one as yet questioned Wyatt's taste, his somewhat trying personality and working habits probably sowed the seeds for his humiliation at the hands of James Loch and the Sutherlands. As early as July 1827, his dilatory ways and lack of initiative irritated Lady Stafford. By August 1829 she found him "not at all an economical architect in the lesser matters". It is true that Loch may have written to Wyatt on 25 June 1829: "... I much wished to have congratulated you on ... the entire magnificence of the finest thing certainly of the kind in

Plate 21
A.C. ROBERTS RA (1796–1864),
Principal Staircase of Stafford House,
1832, oil on canvas, London,
Government Collection of Works of
Art. Note the absence of the large
Veronese copies painted by Giuseppe
Gallo Lorenzi (*fl.* 1840s) between 1841
and 1846. The sculptor of the statue is
unknown, but the work probably
represents *Jonah and the Whale*,
mentioned as being in the hall in the
1833 inventory.

Europe."[81] However, in the end Lady Stafford had the last word: "In spite of
Wyatt's taste and ability I do not think I c'd in conscience recommend him."[82]

The story of the building of Stafford House was resumed barely a week after
the death (on 19 July 1833) of Lord Stafford (or the 1st Duke of Sutherland, as he
had been for the last six months of his life). If there was any possibility of finishing
the building, Benjamin Wyatt was desperately angling for the job. With indelicate

haste, he wrote to James Loch: "I am equally sensible that my object may be lost ... by being an hour too late." Five days later he wrote in the same breathless tone: "I am very anxious to avoid obtruding myself but ... I am desirous not to incur the risk of failing in my object for being *too late* in my application."[83] In all fairness, his attempts to bale his brother Philip out of bankruptcy in 1832 had landed him in the King's Bench Prison for Debtors for a brief but sufficiently humiliating spell. If only he could be allowed to complete Stafford House, his reputation might be salvaged. Without waiting for a reply, he wrote in a similar vein to the 2nd Duke of Sutherland: unaware of her true feelings, he even invoked old Lady Stafford, now known as the Duchess Countess of Sutherland: surely she would have a good word to say for him.[84] But to no avail. Even if the new duke needed to make alterations to Stafford House in order to accommodate his young, growing family of six children, he was not to be rushed into any hasty decisions. Furthermore, he must have taken note of his father's friend Thomas Grenville's damning comparisons with Wyatt's other famous building in St James's, Crockford's Gaming Club:

> Wyat's [*sic*] plans of decoration are probably as costly as he could make them, & latterly the more so ... on account of the Versailles ornaments adopted so foolishly at Crockford's; I suppose his Rule of Three suggests to him that if such decorations are fit for a Club House, those of your Palace must be proportionately more costly: & so they might if you kept a hazard table with high-seasoned supper as a decoy, but till you do I don't see why Stafford House should take Crockford's for its model in decorations.[85]

Meanwhile, Loch sounded out the Edinburgh engineer George Rennie[86] on the possibility of employing Sir Robert Smirke (who had been knighted in 1832) – a choice he would warmly recommend, as there was "no one more capable of executing Buildings or whose works are better done".[87] Up till now, the duke had shown little enthusiasm for Smirke: he even referred to Eastnor Castle as "a Saxon Bastille".[88] But even if Smirke was not necessarily the most inspiring architect of his generation, he was well known for keeping within his estimates: when about to embark on extensive and costly building programmes, such as Stafford House, who better to employ? At the same time, Benjamin Wyatt, an architect renowned for his good taste, had begun the building and he seemed desperate to complete it, so would it not be both kind and logical to assign him the most conspicuous and prestigious part, namely the State Apartments, as long as the costs were reined in? This seems to have been Sutherland's tortuous way of thinking at the time. Indeed, when he wrote to inform Wyatt of his decision, he tried to sugar the pill by referring to the "satisfaction which its being known that you have been the author may well occasion".[89]

But Wyatt was not to be fooled. Indeed, the thought of playing second fiddle to the very architect he had supplanted eight years earlier could only fill him with "mortification",[90] but his straitened circumstances and dwindling practice left him with no choice. His brother Philip tried to solicit the commission, giving rise to an irate letter to the duke from Benjamin[91] belittling his role in the building – and with justification from about 1828. Since Philip was a bankrupt, Sutherland declined his offer, although he was later to remark that he probably deserved more credit than his elder brother was prepared to give him.[92] In his resentment at such a humiliation, Benjamin Wyatt kept his communication with Smirke to a minimum throughout, occasionally addressing stiff and formal letters in the third person: he preferred dealing directly with the duke and duchess. Even the comparatively equable Smirke gave vent to his feelings from time to time. Early on he let it be known that he thought Wyatt's designs for the new exterior "useless" and those for the roof "injudicious".[93] In a letter giving a brief progress report at the end of 1834, Smirke missed no opportunity in telling his employers that the State Apartments were "the only part of the work that has in any way been troublesome but I dare say may *soon* be otherwise".[94] Indeed, they were the only area where he did not have total control.

The division of labour between the two architects was to be as follows: Wyatt was to concern himself with the State Apartments on the first floor (the Picture Gallery, Ante-Rooms, Great South Drawing Room and State Dining Room) and Smirke was responsible for the rest. This meant, in Smirke's case, adding a new storey to accommodate a growing family, and building new kitchen offices in the north-east corner of the Garden Front[95] (pp. 6–7) as the duke did not want a kitchen, nor the smells that went with it, inside the building.[96] While the duchess was to have the run of the equivalent area on the floor above, the duke took over the ground-floor apartments along the west front: these included his own wardrobe, dressing room, small dining room and library.[97] As architect in charge, Smirke's commission on his own work stood at 5% and at 2½% on Wyatt's. He controlled the finances and was in charge of the Clerk of Works, but he interfered little with Wyatt, for all the latter's assertions to the contrary.[98]

Smirke's work on the first and ground floor, as well as the kitchen offices, was completed by the end of 1835. In the early stages, the Sutherlands partly lodged at Bridgewater House, by then the property of the duke's younger brother Lord Francis (created Earl of Ellesmere in 1846); when they could move in, they temporarily settled themselves on the ground floor, with their children in the first-floor apartments intended for themselves.[99] However, by December 1834 Loch was able to write to Sutherland about "astonishing progress": the new rooms were "really excellent and finished with much good taste", and the basement story "nearly finished and a vast improvement to the House".[100] By this time Loch was "in admiration of Smirke", but less enthusiastic about Charles Barry and his work at Trentham Park – "I confess I rather tremble for him".[101] Although the work executed to his designs was largely completed by 1836, Smirke remained as architect in charge until Lady Day 1840. He preferred to leave furniture to the upholsterer, such as Desiré Dellier of Berner Street and George Morant & Son of New Bond Street, and concentrated more on the exteriors. His most conspicuous contributions were to create the top storey and the outside kitchen in the south-east corner (pp. 6–7). The new storey may have taken away the palatial air so admired by the *Literary Gazette*, and it caused his predecessor's pediments, other than that on the North Portico, to be lopped off (*pl. 13*). All in all, this was a harmonious and pleasing but hardly adventurous work.

Between 1833 and 1838 Benjamin Wyatt concerned himself with the lavishly gilt State Apartments on the first floor. In addition to running an office staffed by four clerks, he supervised the execution of his Louis XIV decorations by Bernasconi & Co., the plasterers, and George Jackson & Son, suppliers of "Paste Composition". From the start, Wyatt strongly recommended Jackson's "Paste Composition", a mixture of whiting, linseed oil, gum and resin,[102] as a tough but cheap substitute for wood carving or imported French boiserie. He assured his clients that such decorations in the Waterloo Gallery at Apsley House looked "just as thin ... and delicate as any carving in wood".[103] Indeed, according to Wyatt, "there is not anybody who can do it so well as Jackson of Rathbone Place".[104] His recommendation was acted upon, and Jackson worked extensively in the State Apartments, supplying gilt Louis XIV pier glasses and wall decorations, until the work was finally completed. Wyatt praised the "lightness, sharpness and relief" of paste composition, and on one occasion singled out "the beautiful execution of the Ivy ornament" in the South-West Drawing Room (*pl. 1*).[105] Not that he always championed Jackson: he found his slowness and frequently defective models so irksome that on one occasion he threatened to place his works "into the hands of the plasterer".[106] That role was carried out by Bernasconi, whose men worked on shallow-relief friezes such as the berry and palm-leaf patterns, scrolls and ceiling ornaments throughout the State Apartments. Wyatt would not use them for more intricate work, citing the scroll frieze of the South-West Drawing Room as "thick, solid and 'bunged up'" (*pl. 22*).[107] Nevertheless, unlike Jackson, Bernasconi gave Wyatt "no unnecessary trouble".[108]

Because of Wyatt's anomalous position as designer of the State Apartments but not architect in charge of the works, he left an unprecedentedly detailed bill of both his own and his clerks' drawings.[109] However, none of the 560 drawings have been traced – indeed, they were mostly lost by 1861 – nor were they itemized in numerical order in the bill. Nevertheless, this document helps establish which architect did what. Wyatt was producing designs for – and the builders working in – all rooms of the State Apartments at much the same time. When the 1839 inventory had been compiled, the south and west elevations were fully furnished, but the Picture Gallery, State Dining Room and North-East Ante-Room remained incomplete.[110] Nevertheless, the Picture Gallery had received Guercino's *St Chrysogonus Being Borne by Angels* (*pl. 2*) from Bridgewater House soon after December 1834, so presumably the new lantern was ready to take it by then.[111]

By March 1837 the South-West Drawing Room had been hung with green velvet silk from Lyon (hence its other name, the Green Velvet Room), and by June it was virtually complete: Richard Westmacott had been paid £266. 18s. 0d. for his *Winter and Autumn* chimney piece (*pl. 99*), and Henry Howard 800 guineas for his ceiling painting *The Solar System* (*pl. 108*).[112] A year later (7 June 1838) this "beautifully fitted room" was ready to receive Queen Victoria for the christening of Lady Victoria Leveson-Gower, to whom she was godmother. Consternation was caused when the Archbishop of York nearly dropped the baby, but the queen enjoyed a "most elegant luncheon in a beautiful new room, which had never been opened to this day" – the Great South Drawing Room (*pl. 32*) – and she was struck by the use of flowers to frame the looking-glasses – done with "the prettiest effect possible".[113]

In March 1837 Desiré Dellier, the main upholsterer, was replaced by George Morant & Son, whose firm had long been painting and gilding Stafford House as well as festooning the looking glasses with flowers for Queen Victoria's visit:[114] the former's furniture covered all manner of styles, and his most conspicuous item was the Louis XIV case of a piano, placed in the foreground of the Picture Gallery in Bedford Lemère's photographs of 1895 (*pl. 23*).[115] James Loch described Dellier as an "arrant scoundrel" after he had fled to Brussels to elude his creditors, having tried among other things to fob them off with some chairs for which the Sutherlands had already paid. Morant's furnishings consisted mostly of white and gold Louis XIV furniture, much of it upholstered in amber-coloured silk. As well as making a folding screen to incorporate some small Watteau paintings,[116] they supplied Duchess Harriet's bathroom with a cabinet "composed of Dolphins, Bull rushes and finished with white & Gold". Perhaps Morant's most monumental piece was a large table, with a marble top and the frame made up of carved swans and lotuses, made for the South-West Drawing Room. It was later reproduced in the *Art Journal*'s illustrated catalogue to the Great Exhibition of 1851 as "from a design furnished by the Duchess of Sutherland".[117] Morant's most conspicuous pieces still *in situ* are the pier tables, with "groups of Italian carved figures … smoothed as Statuary Marble", in the Great South Drawing Room (*pl. 24*). All of

these (bar the screen, which was delivered a year earlier) were supplied in 1838.[118]

By 1837 James Loch was becoming alarmed at the extent to which the building
costs at Trentham and Stafford House were consuming Sutherland capital. The
duke's annual income was about £90,000, but both he and his wife were addicted
to building, and to a far greater extent than his father, who annually earned over
twice as much. Under Smirke's management, the simple building costs at Stafford
House amounted to about £75,000. By the time he had signed his last bill (March
1840), the Sutherlands had spent a grand total of £237,153 on the purchase and
subsequent building and decoration; and the final figure would be just under
£250,000.[119] All too aware of a looming lawsuit between Wyatt and the Duke of

Plate 23
Views of the Picture Gallery and lantern, photographed from the south by Bedford Lemère, Stafford House, 1895. The candelabra were probably supplied by Antoine Lynen of Paris. The case of the piano was supplied by Desiré Dellier, the rogue upholsterer, whom Morant replaced in 1836.

Sutherland, Loch wrote in somewhat admonishing tones to Charles Barry, about to take over from Smirke: "I beg you to consider that the eyes of London will be on the duke and through him on you ... and that it is not unlikely that it may also be the discussion in the Courts of Law if Mr Wyatt shall proceed against the Duke for his excessive demand."[120]

Wyatt had left a parting bill for £5872. 14s. 11d., but it was the outstanding sum of almost £1772. 14s. 11d.[121] that particularly rankled with Sutherland. After all, Wyatt had already received £3900, a considerably larger sum than the £2582. 18s. 6d.[122] that Smirke had received as architect in charge, and the duke could be forgiven for thinking his payment "ample".[123] While expressing "surprise" to Wyatt at the amount due, the duke and Loch agreed that the sum was excessive and the method of accounting unprecedented. In all fairness to the duke, Wyatt never presented a single invoice until he left – an anomaly pointed out by Sir Charles Barry.[124] The duke had every reason to assume that he was up to date with his payments, and Loch would later remind Wyatt: "you have already rec'd better than 12 per cent upon the outlay to which Your drawings refer and nearly 7 per cent upon the total expenditure on the House since the duke commenced the work ..." – in other words considerably more than the customary 5% commission that architects could normally expect.[125]

But why turn his back on perhaps his only substantial source of income in his declining years? Wyatt's patience finally snapped: had he not diligently complied with every passing whim his clients might have had? Both Wyatt's bill and his correspondence record a sequence of adopted and then abandoned ideas, such as Corinthian pilasters along the north and south walls,[126] and scagliola dados and marble doorways in the State Dining Room,[127] not to mention the idea of placing above them bas-relief tondos from Paris – "very pretty for a clock", as Wyatt observed.[128] One suggestion, originating from M. Thiers, a French government minister, but cleverly sidestepped by Wyatt, was to use a bronze replica of Ghiberti's *Gates of Paradise* as the north door of the Picture Gallery.[129] Splendid as the idea was, Wyatt wrote, association and location played their part in enhancing the original, and although the north end of the Picture Gallery was the best place for them, they would still look rather out of place.[130] The duke conceded the point.

However, neither would compromise over the question of the lantern of the Picture Gallery, a contentious issue that had blown up in about November 1837. The duke was becoming increasingly dissatisfied with the slope of the piers, and claimed the authority of a fictitious French architect to insist that they should be placed upright and not on an incline, as they had been for the last three years. This provoked the somewhat surprising outburst from Wyatt that "there is no weaker authority than a French Architect".[131] The seeds of doubt may have been

Plate 24
Pier table with "groups of Italian carved figures ... smoothed as Statuary Marble" (detail), in the former State Drawing Room (Great South Drawing Room), Lancaster House, supplied in 1838 by George Morant & Son.

sown by a young Rothschild from Paris, who criticized the sloping caryatids in the lantern of the Principal Staircase. Thomas Grenville may have dismissed him in retrospect as a "pert monkey [such as] a rich young Frenchman is sure to be!"[132] but doubts persisted. In the event, the Picture Gallery lantern was taken down and the original piers – pilasters decorated with garlands and husks – were dispensed with. Much to Wyatt's chagrin, Charles Barry – whom he later suspected of being that "French Architect" – had them replaced with gilt palm trees and dates, which he himself had designed (*pl. 2*). Following the disagreements over the Picture Gallery lantern and his supersession by Charles Barry, Wyatt resigned in June 1838 rather than face dismissal. "Greatly mortified" as he felt, he claimed "neither the Right nor the Inclination … to murmur at Your Grace's decision".[133]

The duke refused to pay the bill that followed, so Wyatt eventually resorted to a barrister by the name of Harrison and sued for the outstanding amount. The lawsuit was heard intermittently in the Lincoln's Inn chambers of Sir Walter Ridell QC from 15 February 1841 until 20 April 1842, when judgment was finally passed in favour of Wyatt. The latter's case highlighted what the duchess had euphemistically called "our difficulties of decision", ranging from the replicas of Lorenzo Ghiberti's *Gates of Paradise* to the final falling-out over the Picture Gallery lantern. The duke's case rested on the fact that Wyatt's method of charging (namely, by time rather than commission percentage) was unprecedented. He had already received more than Sir Robert Smirke, the architect in charge, while doing only half the work, and many of his drawings included in the bill were unnecessary: up to a third of the coloured drawings could have been done just as well in pencil, and a third also were copied from those for Apsley House.[134]

First of all, Wyatt's barrister managed to establish that wives' letters (in this case, those of the Duchess of Sutherland) were admissible evidence. Then he could proceed to list her frequent changes of mind, and go on to prove that Wyatt and his clerks had squandered twice as much time on unused drawings than those that served any practical purpose. The Sutherlands' barrister failed to undermine the reliability of the clerks' time books or indeed their recollections of Wyatt: they all agreed that he was a meticulous supervisor, who never supplied any superfluous drawings. All those questioned repeatedly emphasized the elaborate and time-consuming nature of Louis XIV decoration, and that in a similar position they too would be able to charge only by time. Charging this way was quite legitimate: William Coleman, a former clerk and now a practising architect, had done so with his (untraced) "Double Houses" in Fulham. Likewise Alexander Dick Gough, Wyatt's former chief clerk, with Vice-Chancellor James Knight Bruce's house, the Priory, Roehampton. Perhaps the most telling point was that commission percentages depended on the cost of materials, and Wyatt's elaborate drawings were mostly applied to cheap materials such as Jackson's putty. By charging that way, Wyatt would have lost out. It was left to Thomas Hopper to vindicate Wyatt: in his view, these charges were, if anything, "cutting it close", and the architect of Penrhyn Castle observed with gentle irony that the duchess was "a Lady of such known taste in ornamental decorations that ... she would very frequently be suggesting certain things which would require great additional labour".

On the strength of the evidence before him, Ridell awarded Wyatt the £1776 outstanding and costs at about £540. The duchess raged at "the most preposterous decision" in favour of "so wanton and unnecessary an architect",[135] whereas her husband played the good loser and conceded that "little annoyances of the sort are perhaps rather wholesome!" Wyatt scored a pyrrhic victory. Even if he was able to live off his award, he is not known to have received any substantial commissions after the trial. Indeed, he had made so many enemies in his profession that his death in 1855 went unrecorded in the journals that a generation earlier would have praised his taste. Nevertheless, it is Benjamin Dean Wyatt that later generations of architects must thank for not having to rely entirely on the 5% commission and for being legally entitled to charge for designs for unexecuted work.

But what of Charles Barry's role (*pl. 25*) in all of this? By September 1838 Wyatt was in no doubt as to his "meddling in a way which I think was very unfair and improper to me".[136] How justified was his complaint? Up until September 1838 Barry without doubt played the role of unofficial architectural *arbiter elegantiae* to the Sutherlands during Wyatt's employment at Stafford House. As early as 1833 they were captivated by his taste and extensive knowledge, not to mention his outstanding ability as a draughtsman. Indeed, Barry had travelled and studied extensively not only in France but also in Italy, Sicily and the Middle East – something that was bound to appeal to such cosmopolitan patrons as the Sutherlands. In contrast, Wyatt's opportunity for travel would have been severely limited in his early professional career. Once hostilities had finally ceased with France, he seems to have confined himself, with the exception of a brief visit to Italy in 1818,[137] largely to the Ile-de-France. By November 1833 we find Barry being invited by the Duchess Countess of Sutherland to dinner at Hamilton Place to show off his collections of drawings made on his trip to Egypt (September 1818 – March 1819).[138] Wyatt never enjoyed such intimacy.

Charles Barry first swam into the Sutherlands' ken when Francis Chantrey recommended him to make designs for a pedestal for a funerary monument to the 1st duke at their property at Lilleshall, Shropshire, in October 1833.[139] The Sutherlands were captivated by what Loch was later to call "his beautiful facility for drawing which makes him a very dangerous adviser both to himself and his employers".[140] In October 1833 Barry was commissioned to rebuild the duke's main

Plate 25
JOHN PRESCOTT KNIGHT (1803–1881), *Sir Charles Barry*, 1851, oil on canvas, London, National Portrait Gallery. Barry was knighted in 1851, largely for his work on the Houses of Parliament. Until his final dispute with the Sutherlands over a bill concerning work done at Cliveden in 1855, Barry was their favourite architect. He finished off the work of Wyatt and Smirke at Stafford House but worked extensively at Trentham, Staffordshire; Cliveden, Buckinghamshire; and to a lesser extent at Dunrobin Castle, Sutherland.

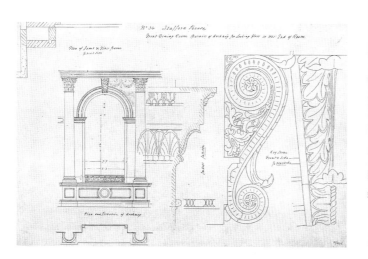

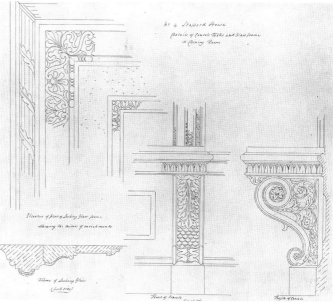

English seat, Trentham, Staffordshire, in the Italianate style and create new gardens there. Such an undertaking would seriously dent their resources, enormous as they were, and drive Loch in September 1838 to utter a dire warning: "at the present moment you are not living within your income, and by the time that the great outlay at Stafford House & Trentham is over, your income will be diminished permanently while your expenditure in every way will be increased."[141] Earlier that year, he had likened Barry to John Nash: "he varies too much from his original works ... and he is too great a suggester of new work."[142] This very fault Loch was to emphasize when he wrote to the architect in April 1839: "your genius and talent make you a dangerous person to trust in an old House for every time you revisit it you see something to improve – I am in the less agreeable situation of grudging every sixpence that is spent unnecessarily."[143] Notwithstanding Loch's admonitions, over £72,000 had been spent at Trentham by 1842, and work was to continue for the rest of the decade. Nevertheless, the Sutherlands regarded Barry as a genius,[144] and attempted to reassure both themselves and Loch that all would be well.[145]

Barry did not limit his attentions to Trentham Park. Indeed, as early as December 1833, Sutherland was writing to Loch: "we are much pleased with Mr Barry's taste – which is certainly far superior to B. Wyatt's and I think will be of use to us in many respects about finishing at Stafford House, where we are not satisfied with Wyatt."[146] Furthermore, in an undated letter of that period, Sutherland mentioned asking Barry to visit Stafford House, "as he does not know the Great Rooms & his task will be very useful in our consideration of Wyatt's designs".[147] Nevertheless, until the fictitious "French" architect made his appearance in November 1837, Wyatt seems to

Plate 26 (top left)
After CHARLES BARRY (1795–1860), *No. 34. Stafford House, Great Dining Room. Details of Archway for Looking Glass at West End of Room* [*i.e.* State Dining Room, also known as the Banqueting Room], 21 April 1846, ink on paper, London, Royal Institute of British Architects. Despite the late date on the drawing, Charles Barry was working on this room between 1839 and 1840.

Plate 27 (top right)
Attr. CHARLES BARRY (1795–1860), *No. 4 Stafford House/Details of Console Tables and Glass frame in Dining Room*, *c.* 1846, ink on paper, London, Royal Institute of British Architects. The "Dining Room" referred to is the ground-floor Dining Room, which Charles Barry modified between 1839 and 1840.

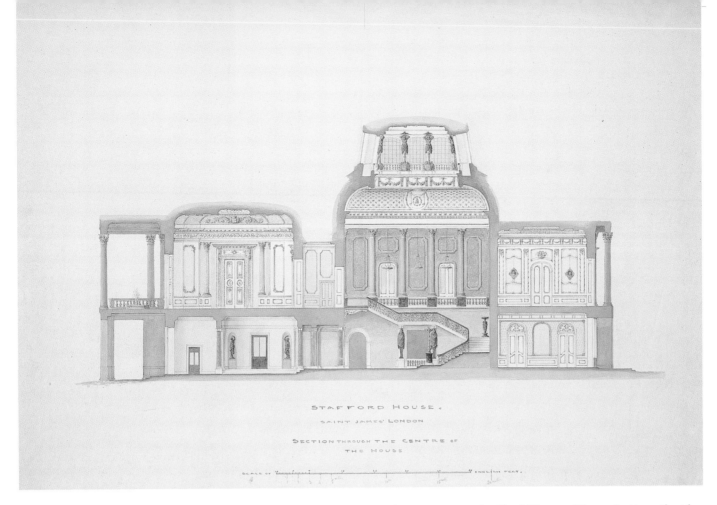

STAFFORD HOUSE.

SAINT JAMES' LONDON

SECTION THROUGH THE CENTRE OF
THE HOUSE

Plate 28
After CHARLES BARRY (1795–1860),
*Stafford House, Saint James' London.
Section through the Centre of the House*,
c. 1839, ink on paper, London, Museum
of London. Charles Barry had been
encouraged to study the designs of
Stafford House as early as 1833, but this
drawing was most likely executed soon
after he took over as architect in charge
in September 1839.

have remained unaware of Barry's activities at Stafford House. The only time that he
is known to have commented on another architect's alterations to his drawings he
was in no doubt that Smirke was responsible.[148]

Satisfied or not, the Sutherlands kept Wyatt working on his designs for almost
five years and, at the same time, contending with their constant changes of mind.
To what extent Barry was changing their minds for them remains a matter for
speculation. Few of the duke's letters, which gave rise to Wyatt's laboured
answers, survive. One of them (undated) referred to an anonymous suggestion
that the outer wall of the Great South Drawing Room (pp. 6–7) be brought out
to the exterior columns, thus converting them into three-quarter columns, and
thereby removing the temptation for children to climb out on to the space in front
of the windows. Wyatt, who later succeeded in dissuading the duke, scribbled on
the back: "this letter contains what, to a Duke or Duchess, is a 'very good
suggestion' but in practical architecture would amount to an absurdity."[149]
However, there is no sign of any curiosity as to just whose idea it was. Whatever
the Sutherlands' original intentions may have been, cast-iron evidence of
interference on the part of Barry remains elusive. Any suggestions he might have
made would have come to Wyatt through the duke and duchess, and thus have
been regarded as the sacrosanct wishes – in theory, at any rate – of the client, and
not the meddling of another architect. Furthermore, the Sutherlands felt that

they had to be discreet – it was the opinion of fictitious French architects they referred to: never once did they mention Barry's name. One suspects that if they had consulted their favourite architect as frequently as they had originally intended, then Wyatt's suspicions would no doubt have been aroused earlier. No doubt work on the new Houses of Parliament, not to mention at Trentham, and to a lesser extent Dunrobin, left him with precious little time to cause trouble.

When the time came to take on the mantle of architect in charge, Barry occupied that position for a relatively short time. Although Loch entrusted the work to him in September 1839, Smirke ceased signing admeasurements only after 31 March 1840. No formal letter of resignation from Smirke has surfaced – and perhaps none was written. However, he withdrew, partly owing to his "troublesome rheumatism or gout"[150] and partly owing to the prospect of extensive alterations to the State Dining Room (*pl. 64*) – and the virtual rebuilding of the north front as a result.[151] Barry signed two admeasurements, the last one dated 31 December 1841.[152] But a letter of 14 December 1841 discussing the salary of John Fish, the clerk of works by then fully responsible for the building, refers to Barry finishing work in July 1841.[153] However, Barry was still signing separate bills as late as April 1842, even if his role had shifted to Trentham and (to a lesser extent) Dunrobin.

Loch feared that under Barry costs at Stafford House would spiral out of control. His letter of 13 September 1839 informing the architect of his new role is more one of admonishment than congratulation.[154] He could, however, console himself that the idea of "lowering and raising some mirrors by machinery" had been dropped. After all, as Loch observed, "it would not have been considered as consistent with the decorum and dignity of the manners of one of our ancient nobility". In the event neither of Barry's two admeasurements[155] exceeded those of Sir Robert Smirke. Barry's work is conspicuous but largely confined to the State Dining Room (*pl. 64*), Picture Gallery (*pls. 2, 62*) and ground-floor Dining Room (*pl. 29*). His initial brief was to take down the north front of the State Dining Room so as to enlarge the windows; expand the entrance of the hall into the corridors; and raise the floor of the hall so as to do away with the steps nearest the entrance.[156] In addition, much of Barry's work was to supervise the execution of Wyatt's designs, and that amounted to half the cost of his admeasurements.[157]

Alterations in the State Dining Room were triggered by falling plaster under the portico in March 1839, which revealed rotten timbers.[158] Nevertheless, little was done until October.[159] But two months later the rotting timbers in the State Dining Room had been removed, walls were cut away for panelling and the bricklayers were altering the windows. Judging from George Jackson's bills, Barry was largely responsible for the design and decoration of the monumental doors on the south and east walls (*pls. 64, 67*),[160] as well as the fine double "S" decoration to

Wyatt's arched recess[161] and ornate dado decoration at the west end of the State Dining Room. Barry's work in the Lower Dining Room consisted of simple, rectangular panelling for the walls, and pairs of gilt pier glasses and white and gilt sideboards with massive consoles (*pls. 27, 29*), the former executed by George Jackson and Son.[162] By November 1839 the panelling was completed and awaited painting.[163]

From January 1839 Barry saw to the installation of figured, embossed glass work, designed by John Henning, Jr, for the lantern of the Picture Gallery (*pl. 84*).[164] The other work by Henning (whose most conspicuous work is perhaps the frieze à la Parthenon on the outside of the Athenaeum) included the sculpted reliefs of Murillo to be placed in the recesses above the recently acquired Marshal Soult's Murillos (*pl. 30*),[165] and the decoration of the large mirrors at both the north and south ends of the Picture Gallery with strips of embossed glass in the Italian Renaissance style, in the form of pilasters (*pl. 83*).[166] Henning's last contribution was to design and model in 1842 four monumental – but, sadly, untraced – marble-topped side tables, assembled by George Jackson & Son,[167] one in each corner of the State Dining Room (*pl. 31*).

By January 1842 the State Apartments were finally completed; in 1844 Barry built stables[168] between Little St James's Street and Cleveland Row, on the site of those that had formerly belonged to Lord Harrington.[169] (These purely functional and unadorned buildings were executed for the comparatively modest sum of £2387. 17s. 11d.).[170] However, Barry's position as the Sutherlands' favourite architect did not last for ever. The roots of the final quarrel lay in the acquiring of Cliveden House, Buckinghamshire, in July 1849, for which the Sutherlands paid £40,000.[171] A mere four months afterwards, the building went up in flames, and during the subsequent

rebuilding, relations between the Sutherlands and Barry cooled. By then, they were paying more heed to James Loch's grim prognostications on the long-term future of their finances, and Barry's tendency to exceed his estimates was treated with less indulgence. Indeed, by March 1854, he had gone just over £12,600 above the original contract of £16,000.[172] The duchess tried to conceal the amounts being spent,[173] and the duke was enraged at, among other things, Barry's ordering of some very expensive chimney pieces without his permission.[174] In an atmosphere of increasing froideur, it was an untraced bill for £1485. 13s. od., presented in January 1855, that caused the final parting between Barry and the Sutherlands.[175] It was the (unspecified) charge for the positioning of a statue of Joan of Arc by Princess Marie-Christine d'Orléans (1813–1839) that particularly irritated the duke – it cost more than the object itself.[176] The Sutherlands may subsequently have taken to referring to *Sir* Charles Barry (he was knighted in 1851) in distinctly sarcastic tones; the duchess, in the company of Queen Victoria, may have cut Barry dead at a Royal Academy opening; but she made at least one discreet enquiry through George Loch as to the state of his health in December 1857,[177] and she is reported as "weeping like a child" at the sight of his grave in 1860.[178]

Architects' souls may have been "lost to the Kingdom of Heaven" in the process of building Stafford House. Nevertheless, by 1842 the grandest town house had

finally been completed, and was to serve as the nerve centre of social life in London throughout Victoria's reign. All three architects were to some extent battered and bruised by this commission – in particular Wyatt. Nevertheless, all three – particularly Wyatt – could point with pride at their great œuvre at the bottom of Green Park, the greatest palace for a nobleman in the smartest part of London.

2 "The Revived Taste of Louis the Fourteenth"

No visitor can fail to be struck by the unashamedly opulent decoration of the inside of Lancaster House. Whether considered to be the height of good taste or the depths of vulgarity, those interiors, intended to hark back to the splendours of Louis XIV's court at Versailles, are certainly memorable. What was referred to as the Louis XIV style from about 1825 was in fact the earliest form of Rococo revival, a style more readily associated with grand hotels or *fin-de-siècle* brothels than the town houses of the English ruling classes in the decades that followed the Battle of Waterloo. In those days, anyone with the necessary resources could pay his money and take his choice as to the style for any room in his house, be it Grecian, Gothic, Egyptian or whatever, and still be regarded as highly fashionable. The most lavish and unashamedly patrician style available was Louis XIV, "suitable to the kingly palace, as it is to the mansion of the nobleman", in the view of George Smith.[1] Whatever associations it was later to acquire, in its earliest stages the Louis XIV style was regarded as aristocratic: indeed, Prince Pückler-Muskau was to observe after a visit to Crockford's Gaming Club in 1828: "Everything is now in the revived taste of Louis the Fourteenth, decorated with tasteless excrescences, excess of gilding ... a turn of fashion very consistent in a country where the nobility grows more and more like that of the time of Louis the Fourteenth."[2] At the time the German prince was writing, no residences could have been grander than Londonderry House, Stafford House or Apsley House, the three London houses that most typified Louis XIV decoration; and at Crockford's, one was sure to meet young rakes, all of them bent on gambling away their inheritances.

But what exactly is the Louis XIV style and how did it get its name? Although Louis XIV and his palace at Versailles provided the main source of inspiration, the term is something of a misnomer. Far from religiously copying French Baroque – the style that prevailed in France during the reign of Louis XIV (1651–1715) – such professional architects as the Wyatts and such gifted amateurs as Earl de Grey

Plate 32
Former State Drawing Room (also known as the Great South Drawing Room), Lancaster House. The wall decoration and pier glass frames were supplied by George Jackson & Son and the pier tables by George Morant & Son.

51

freely borrowed any element they fancied from such works as Jean Mariette's *L'Architecture françoise* (Paris 1735–38) or Germain Boffrand's *Livre d'architecture* (Paris 1745). 'Louis XIV' was an evocative and at the same time highly convenient term to use – whether accurate or not – and Benjamin Wyatt was using it as early as November 1825. The fact that Charles Cockerell, an architect who had no connection with Wyatt, was also using it by December 1826 would suggest that it was fairly widespread by then. It must be conceded that the use of Rococo never really died in ceramics and metalwork – in 1812 the goldsmiths Rundell, Bridge & Rundell made tureens "from the pattern of the Duke of Orleans".[3] Furthermore, inlaid tortoiseshell and gilt brass furniture contemporary with the work of André-Charles Boulle was much sought after, and pieces inspired by this particular style enjoyed a vogue in England under the name of Buhl from the 1790s. Between 1811 and 1814 Sir Jeffry Wyattville (or Jeffry Wyatt, as he then was) restored Isaac Ware's Rococo interiors of Chesterfield House (*pl. 33*), and employed the talents of his cousin, Edward Wyatt, to match the original Rococo carving or produce something similar. Nevertheless, with the exception of Buhl, the Rococo revival in furniture and interiors did not really begin until 1824, when the Rutlands acquired boiserie, which was said to have come from a château that had formerly belonged to Mme de Maintenon, morganatic wife of Louis XIV from 1684.

War never put a stop to French fashions in England. Throughout the hostilities, French decorative painters such as Jean-Jacques Boileau and Alexandre Louis Delabrière, and hosts of cabinetmakers of French extraction, made a good living without any hindrance or persecution. Thomas Hope's extensive borrowing from and acknowledgement of his debt to Percier and Fontaine in his *Household Interior Decoration* (London 1807) may have attracted mild criticism from a few commentators, but his engravings were freely adapted by upholsterers and cabinetmakers. Once the Universal Peace had been established in 1814, Paris, and indeed Versailles, became easily accessible to English travellers and pleasure-seekers. But it was Napoleon rather than Louis XIV who initially captured their imagination. Those who wrote down their experiences were most forcibly struck by the extreme luxury in which the deposed emperor had once wallowed. Benjamin Haydon wrote after a visit to Fontainebleau: "No palace of any sultan of Baghdad or monarch of India ever exceeded the voluptuous magnificence of these apartments."[4] Frances, Lady Shelley wrote of St Cloud: "The luxury of this palace exceeds every idea I had formed of Parisian extravagance. The gallery is at once the richest, and most beautiful realization of Arabic splendour that can be imagined."[5] When it came to copying what the French had to offer, it was the engravings of Charles Percier and Pierre Fontaine, rather than surviving pieces of French Baroque furniture, that caught the attention of such upholsterers as Morel and Hughes or indeed the fashion plates of *Ackerman's Repository*.[6]

However, a different view was taken by Elizabeth, Duchess of Rutland, who wrote an account of her visit to Paris and Versailles in July 1814.[7] She expressed a strong preference for the pre-Napoleonic sections of St Cloud: "in the Gallery and salon, the ancient ceilings remain untouched, and they are superb." At Versailles she was particularly impressed by the ceilings painted by Le Brun.[8] Nevertheless, another ten years were to pass before the duchess created a Louis XIV interior at Belvoir Castle. Following the fire of 1816, the Rutlands chose the Gothic and Neo-classical styles for their redecoration. But for the fortuitous availability of some French boiserie in July 1824, the Elizabeth Saloon (*pl. 34*) might never have been created and the Louis XIV style could have taken a very different form. But because of the Mme de Maintenon associations, panelling that later generations would have recognized as Rococo was regarded instead as perhaps the best relic of the epoch of Louis XIV that anyone could ever want.

In June 1824 the Duchess of Rutland asked Colonel Trench to show her what she called "the Madame de Maintenon Furniture".[9] Two months later her husband bought it from Matthew Cotes Wyatt, Benjamin's younger brother, for 1450 guineas, and work began.[10] The boiserie was assembled by a Mr Alcock, described as a "really very clever and very accurate … young man",[11] and an extra dado constructed by a carpenter called Armstrong, because the panels were too short.[12] The Elizabeth Saloon's most Baroque feature – in spirit if not in style – was the ceiling painting of the myth of Io: M.C. Wyatt depicted the Duchess of Rutland as Juno (earlier, he had somewhat tactlessly suggested she should be Io, who, as everyone knew, got turned into a cow), the Duke of York in the guise of Mercury, and Argus, no doubt, represented the hostile press, bent on undermining Trench's

Thames Quay schemes. The Duchess of Rutland had designed the ceiling, in the form of three converging lunettes and a roundel, with portraits of the duke, duchess, their children and Colonel Trench inserted in the spaces between. No doubt she arrived at this unorthodox solution by misinterpreting the lunettes placed above cornices in engraved architectural cross-sections. Finished by January 1829, it was hailed by Harriet Arbuthnot as "the most magnificent room I ever saw, fitted up in the style of Louis XIV in panels of blue silk damask & the most beautiful carving and gilding".[13]

The provenance of the boiserie remains uncertain: the Revd Irwin Eller, in his detailed account of Belvoir Castle, says they came from an unspecified château of Mme de Maintenon.[14] However, the duke told Lady Shelley that they had come from "Madame de Maintenon's apartment in the Trianon [presumably at Versailles]". It is now thought that they were probably originally made for a grand Parisian town house and date from about 1735, fourteen years or more after Mme de Maintenon's death in 1719.[15] However, the associations are what count: the fact that neither the Rutlands nor their architects saw any reason to doubt the provenance helps explain why so many Rococo features are found in a style called 'Mme de Maintenon' by the Duchess of Rutland and 'Louis XIV' by others. Those involved with the Elizabeth Saloon seem to have been blissfully unaware of any anachronisms that might manifest themselves to later generations. Indeed, soon after the boiserie appeared, the duchess playfully scolded Trench for sending her "the Mme de Maintenon gown" before the saloon was finished, as "surely you would not have me wear it till then".[16]

Where the Rutlands led, others – including royalty – followed: Alexandre Delahante, a Parisian dealer, supplied panelling for the Ballroom of Windsor Castle in 1825; Benjamin Wyatt bought an unspecified and untraced quantity for York House in Paris in 1826;[17] and Lord Stuart de Rothesay did likewise for his Hampshire residence at Highcliffe in about 1834.[18] By September 1833 Benjamin Wyatt was warning the Duke of Sutherland that panels of high quality were expensive "now that the French know that there is a market for such things in England".[19] Even allowing for sales talk on behalf of Jackson's putty, Wyatt's words indicate that eighteenth-century French boiserie, which would have been removed and disposed of a generation earlier, was now much sought after, and not only by a few Francophile fanatics.

Although George IV's schemes for Windsor Castle are chiefly associated in the minds of posterity with A.W.N. Pugin and Gothic Revival, it should not be forgotten that there was also a very strong French flavour to the decoration.[20] The Ballroom was made up of boiserie supplied by Alexandre Delahante in July 1826 for £500. Two Boulle armoires occupied a prominent position in the King's Sitting Room, a

Plate 34

Elizabeth Saloon with ceiling, Belvoir Castle, Leicestershire, 1956. Note the adapted boiseries and the added dado, by a carpenter called Armstrong, on the far right of the picture. The ceiling, with its curious converging circles, was designed by Elizabeth, Duchess of Rutland, Colonel Frederick William Trench and Matthew Cotes Wyatt, Benjamin's younger brother. Note the French 'sagging arch' chimney piece, dating from the 1730s and used by Gilles-Marie Oppenord in the Palais Royal in Paris as early as 1717, later to be freely borrowed by Benjamin Wyatt.

bronze equestrian statuette of Louis XIV in the Gothic Dining Room and four large Gobelins tapestries in the Coffee Room. The king's cabinetmaker, Nicholas Morel, was sent to France in 1826 to collect patterns and drawings of French furniture.[21] After Lord Stafford had acquired York House, it was Morel rather than Benjamin Dean Wyatt whom he consulted on matters concerning furniture. What was good enough for the king was good enough for his richest subject.

Thomas Philip, Earl de Grey (1781–1859) was certainly not one to leave it all to his upholsterer. Indeed, he used his visits to Paris as an opportunity to study French architecture of the preceding century: his written accounts provide us with a unique insight into the activities of an English architectural enthusiast in the French capital during the 1820s.[22] When in 1825 he decided to rebuild Wrest Park, his country house in Bedfordshire, he consulted Colonel John Gurwood, former comrade-in-arms of the Duke of Wellington and editor of the *Despatches*. The Colonel was able to supply de Grey with a list of books to consult in the

Bibliothèque Royale in Paris and names of specialist bookshops, where he eventually managed to find a modestly priced edition of Jean Mariette's *L'Architecture françoise*, which he called his "textbook".[23] Gurwood's familiarity with the subject suggests that there was an increasing interest in French architecture within Wellington's circle, some three years before the creation of that great essay in Louis XIV, the Waterloo Gallery at Apsley House. De Grey never mentioned Wyatt but Gurwood probably knew him well: both were then working closely with the Duke of Wellington, and they may well have swapped information on books on French architecture, and the most likely suppliers in Paris. No doubt at Gurwood's suggestion, Earl de Grey commemorated, in a cartouche in the Staircase Hall, the 'Holy Trinity' of Blondel, Mansart and Le Pautre. These three architects (together with Mariette) were to provide the main sources of inspiration for the Louis XIV style.

Armed with his Parisian 'spoils', Earl de Grey proceeded to rebuild Wrest Park between 1833 and 1839 with the first ever Louis XIV exterior. This he borrowed from Jacques-François Blondel's engravings in *De la distribution des maisons de plaisance* (Paris 1737–38): he curved the tops of the windows and crowned the central section of the building with a flattened dome, in an uncompromisingly Gallic manner. The French spirit remained undimmed inside. Recorded in a series of six undated watercolours of about 1840 by Thomas Scandrett RA (1797–1870),[24] these were largely Rococo confections, based on engravings by Mariette and Blondel: the staircase, with its serpentine railing, is copied from Blondel's engraving *Decoration d'escalier vu sur la largeur*, taken from *De la distribution des maisons de plaisance*. De Grey was not always satisfied with his designs: the ceiling of the Library he thought was "exactly in the form of a fine large turbot". However, he was a rich, talented amateur, able to design whatever he pleased. Fashionable society regarded him as the expert on French architecture. When Lord Ellesmere bought some "*Old French* iron gates" for Worsley Hall, his house in Lancashire, he announced his intention of "calling a counsel as to the best mode of dealing with them with learned men, Gregory of Harlaxton and Lord de Grey".[25]

Louis XIV was not confined to royalty and patrician dilettanti. Indeed it found favour with the oldest City Livery Company, that of the Goldsmiths, when they chose to rebuild their hall in 1833. The architect responsible was Philip Hardwick (1792–1870). His eclecticism ranged from Jacobethan revival at the new hall and library for Lincoln's Inn (completed in 1845) to the uncompromisingly Grecian propylaeum of Euston Station (1837). However, it was Louis XIV that he would choose for the Court Drawing Room of the Goldsmiths' Hall (destroyed 16 April 1941). After becoming their surveyor in 1829, he was called upon by the Goldsmiths to demolish the old premises and build in their place a grand classical

building with a Corinthian hexastyle portico. The Court Drawing Room was executed in the Louis XIV style. His reasons are not recorded but no doubt his employers would have thought an abundance of gilding most fitting – and what better style than Louis XIV?

Fortunately, the Court Drawing Room is recorded in the Bedford Lemère photographs of 1892 (*pl. 35*) and a set of finished drawings in the collections of the Goldsmiths' company. The ceiling, with its enormous central tondo, is taken from Jean Cotelle's *Livre de divers ornemens* (*pl. 36*), and the chimney piece on the east wall is adorned with a sagging arch, a standard Louis XIV element ever since M.C. Wyatt had installed the 'Madame de Maintenon' fireplaces at Belvoir Castle (*pl. 34*). Hardwick seems to have played safe and contented himself with Mariette's *L'Architecture françoise*, but then he was working in very different circumstances from Wyatt. As surveyor of the Goldsmiths' Hall, he had the full trust of his employers; his brief was to complete the new building as quickly as possible and work to the least expensive of two sets of designs.[26]

Where the fashionable led, the engravers soon followed. George Smith included a plate entitled *Interior Decoration Age of Louis XIV* in his *Cabinet-Maker's and Upholsterer's Guide* (London 1826). It was probably based on Benjamin Wyatt's interiors at Crockford's Club, the only example of this style to be mentioned by Smith. "As this mansion is solely appropriated to the nightly purposes of pleasure," he wrote, "perhaps such a taste may be in unison with the wasteful transfer made

Plate 36
JEAN COTELLE (1642–1708), design
(half-plan) for a ceiling, watercolour,
c. 1650, Oxford, Ashmolean Museum of
Art and Archaeology.

of property in such establishments."[27] To what extent Wyatt co-operated with
Smith, if at all, is not known. In 1829 Thomas King included a number of designs
for furniture, consisting of chairs made up of a jumble of 'C' scrolls in the Louis
XIV style, in his publication *The Modern Style of Cabinet Work exemplified*. At about
this time, he also brought out *Specimens of furniture in the Elizabethan & Louis
Quatorze Styles* (London n.d.): the Louis XIV plates owed far more to the English
Rococo designs of the 1750s than anything of the Régence or French Baroque.
Writing in 1826, George Smith saw Chippendale's engravings very much as the first
examples of Louis XIV furniture designs in England.[28] In 1834 an engraver by the
name of Thomas Wheale reissued *Locke, Johnson & Copland's Ornamental Designs*,
a series of engravings that first appeared in the 1750s. This publication was
condemned in the *Architectural Magazine* as "fancy of the most inferior kind of art
… combining into whole lines and forms which have little or no meaning of
themselves".[29] The magazine damningly concluded: "this book is abundantly
cheap which is the best thing we can say of it." Although Louis XIV furniture
enjoyed great popularity from the early 1830s, Wyatt became increasingly
apprehensive about the spreading and vulgarization of his ideas. No doubt such
comments as those in *Architectural Magazine* fuelled his fears.

Unlike A.W.N. Pugin, Benjamin Wyatt had no wish to propagate his designs,
and voiced his fears to the 2nd Duke of Sutherland:

> … it is not much more to Your Grace's interest than to mine that the
> characteristic features of the decorations of Stafford House should be made
> common, by a thousand tasteless and vulgar applications of the same.[30]

At the outset of his career as an architect, Wyatt's designs were, as Lady Shelley
said, based on "pure Greek models"[31] – or, rather, Ancient Roman, judging from

Plate 42
Galerie des Glaces (1678–85),
Versailles, designed by J.H. Mansart
(1646–1708). This great gallery
inspired Benjamin Wyatt's Waterloo
Gallery at Apsley House, London. Note
the twinned consoles linked with swags
in the cove of the ceiling, a recurring
feature in Louis XIV decoration.

Plate 43
PIERRE LE PAUTRE (*c.* 1648–1716),
Rampes, apuis, et balcons de serrurerie,
Paris, *c.* 1700, Paris, Bibliothèque
Nationale. A likely source for Benjamin
Wyatt's designs for the balustrating of
the Principal Staircases at both Apsley
House and Stafford House.

reasons, the inclusion of such a feature, although never to be executed, lends
credence to Lady Shelley's remark, already quoted, about his "ideas in
architecture [being] based on pure Greek models".

Once Lord Stafford had taken possession of York House in 1828 and renamed it
Stafford House, Benjamin Wyatt radically transformed his designs for the Principal
Staircase, and the Louis XIV elements took on a new vitality, borrowing more
from French Baroque. The shrouded male terms by Mazzoni (*pl. 19*) could well
have been taken from an untitled series engraved by Jean Le Pautre (*pl. 40*).
Wyatt's designs for Joseph Bramah & Son's staircase (largely to be repeated at
Apsley House) were based on Pierre Le Pautre's undated engravings of about
1700, *Rampes, apuis, et balcons de serrurerie* (*pls. 43, 103*). Furthermore, Wyatt
adopted bold scagliola schemes, which harked back to the inlaid marble staircases
by Louis Le Vau (1612–1670) and Jules Hardouin Mansart (1646–1708) at
Versailles. By making his flight of stairs diverge against a monumental backdrop
of *giallo antico* scagliola, he no doubt aimed to recreate the impact and scale of
Le Vau's Escalier des Ambassadeurs, destroyed in 1752 but recorded in the
engraving by Chevotet. Wyatt had discussed *giallo antico* with the Duchess of
Rutland but confined its use to the Entrance Hall of York House, so as to prevent
it "from appearing sombre". With the possible exception of Thomas Cundy's
grand staircase at Northumberland House on the Strand (demolished 1874),
scagliola had seldom, if ever, before been applied to wall decoration in England

Plate 44

Jacques-François Blondel (1705–1775), *Decoration d'une salle amanger vüe du côté du buffet et dont les ornemens sont dorez sur un fond blanc*, from *De la distribution des maisons de plaisance*, Paris 1737–38. The narrow *portes de dégagement* (D) may have served partly as a source for the doors of the Green Library of Stafford House.

on such a lavish scale. William Croggon's scagliola embellishments, fashionable as they then were, consisted mainly of pilasters, columns and balustrading. In addition to these more orthodox features, Wyatt had the landing walls covered with *giallo antico*, embellished with *rondona* (a mauve hue) moulding. On this occasion, Wyatt departed from white paint and gilded rocaille, something he would attempt to repeat in the State Dining Room in 1836, only to be frustrated when his clients abandoned the idea.

On the ground-floor State Apartments, Wyatt employed the French Baroque method of articulating the coves of ceilings with paired consoles, as he had first done in the Striped Drawing Room at Apsley House (see below). These had been used by J.H. Mansart in the Galerie des Glaces (*pl. 42*) at Versailles, and they recur throughout the pages of Mariette. A pattern repeatedly found on the borders of Wyatt's ceilings was the palm-and-ribbon frieze. Although no engraved source has yet been traced, the closest parallel is the palm motif framing the lunettes and vault of the Salon de Guerre (*pls. 2, 41, 108*). As with the doorway in the Faubourg Saint-Honoré, Wyatt was inspired by a surviving piece of fabric that he admired, instead of relying on an engraving.

Wyatt surmounted the doors of the lower drawing room with lunettes, which enclosed Baroque cartouches (*pl. 20*). In Pierre Le Pautre's hands they would have framed bold trophies or monograms, as was the case with the doors leading into the Chapel of Versailles. He could have decorated the leaves of the doors with strictly rectangular panelling, à la French Baroque, or the serpentine version, associated with Oppenord and Blondel. In fact, he mostly compromised by

making the inner edges serpentine and the outer ones rectangular, softening each corner with a small rocaille ornament (*pls. 20, 46*). The most curvilinear door panelling is in the Library (*pl. 52*), where each leaf resembles a summarized version of a *porte de dégagement* in the *Decoration d'une salle amanger ...* in Blondel's *De la distribution des maisons de plaisance* (*pl. 44*).

Unlike the other rooms discussed, the Library was partly decorated in the style of eighteenth-century French boiserie. In addition to its "rich green silk damask" hangings,[46] the walls were decorated with pilasters with scalloped ornaments near the bottom, in a manner similar to Jean Baptiste Leroux's Salon de l'Hôtel de Villeroy (*pl. 45*), or indeed Nicolas Pineau's Salle de Compagnie of the Hôtel de Soubise, recorded in Mariette's *L'Architecture françoise*. The swelling and curvaceous chimney piece with its drooping arch, like all of those on the ground-floor apartments at Stafford House (or indeed the Elizabeth Saloon of Belvoir Castle), follows a pattern developed by Robert de Cotte for the Electoral Palace of Bonn (1716–17) or Gilles-Marie Oppenord for the Palais-Royal in Paris (1717). But as it was then believed that the 'Mme de Maintenon' boiserie and chimney pieces at Belvoir had an impeccable provenance, Wyatt would have genuinely thought that he was correctly reproducing the style of Louis XIV. Even if he was familiar with Pierre Le Pautre's rectangular chimney pieces (*pl. 47*), Wyatt's taste was for the curvaceous and flamboyant.

Plate 46
View of the Ante-Drawing Room
(ground floor), photographed by
Bedford Lemére, Stafford House, 1895,
with a relief of General Garibaldi
sculpted by Luigi Fabbrucci, put up in
June 1883 in memory of Garibaldi's
visit to Stafford House in April 1864.

By about 1830, Benjamin Dean Wyatt was at the zenith of his professional career. He could look with pride upon his two Louis XIV masterpieces: the Principal Staircase of Stafford House (*pls. 21, 103*) and the Waterloo Gallery of Apsley House (*pl. 48*). Following his victory at Waterloo in 1815, the Duke of Wellington, as an internationally renowned statesman, needed a grand London house in keeping with his new status, where he could entertain foreign princes and politicians. Inevitably he turned to Benjamin Wyatt, his former private secretary and by now a well-known architect. A grand Waterloo Palace, in the classical style, was dreamt up soon after victory but never executed. Wellington purchased Apsley House from his debt-ridden elder brother Richard, Marquis of Wellesley for £40,000 in November 1816. Wyatt set about restoring and redecorating it, in a richly gilded version of the Neo-classical style, and completed the first-floor drawing rooms by about 1827. Perhaps the earliest manifestation of Louis XIV was the use of paired consoles to decorate the cover of the Striped Drawing Room. As Thomas Dowbiggin & Son were applying silk hangings to its walls in December 1826, the cove must have been completed by then.[47] Colonel John Gurwood, already mentioned in connection with Lord de Grey, may well have suggested the idea.

In about 1828 the duke decided to extend the building to the west to accommodate the new Waterloo Gallery. He also had his residence refaced in Bath stone and embellished with a Corinthian portico, thus making it resemble a smaller version of York (by then Stafford) House, the once-intended residence of his former commander-in-chief. By February 1829 the Principal Staircase of Apsley House was completed: it had been furnished by Joseph Bramah & Sons with gilt-iron balustrading, very similar to that of Stafford House.[48] By March 1830, Thomas Dowbiggin's men were fitting the controversial yellow silk damask hangings to the Gallery, which by then was near completion.[49] In his surviving letters to Wellington, Wyatt referred to various pieces of available French furniture and picture frames that he thought suitable for this type of decoration.[50] Wellington was happy to delegate to his friend Harriet Arbuthnot, who was most enthusiastic about the Louis XIV style, but he ended up raging at Wyatt's inability to stay within his original estimates.[51]

The Waterloo Gallery was probably the largest room that Benjamin Wyatt had been commissioned to design to date. (Any plans he might have had for the York House Gallery (1825–27) had been shelved once ownership passed to Lord Stafford.) Faced with the task of designing a long, flat expanse of ceiling in the Louis XIV style, Wyatt had to muster all his powers of invention. Unfortunately, the grandest ceilings at Versailles are mostly painted with allegories, and even if Wellington's achievements invited decoration of this nature, neither he nor Mrs

Plate 47

Pierre Le Pautre (*c.* 1648–1716), *Moyennes cheminées pour les chambres, c.* 1700, Paris, Bibliothèque Nationale. Despite Benjamin Wyatt's penchant for chimney pieces with sagging arches, French Baroque examples tended to be rectangular.

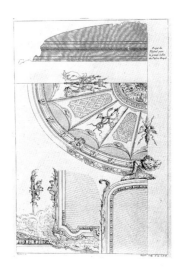

Arbuthnot were interested in the idea. Instead, Wyatt's challenge was both to avoid monotony and illuminate the pictures effectively. Rather than create a large lantern in the centre, Wyatt distributed glass panes and gilded plasterwork throughout the length of the ceiling. The main motifs were a central cupola loosely based on a chinoiserie design by Oppenord (*pl. 50*), flanked by two ceilings made up of intersecting circles, a pattern derived from an unnamed mausoleum published in Robert Wood's *Ruins of Palmyra* (*pl. 51*): in this case, the 'pure Greek' – or rather classical – spirit is seen to reassert itself in Wyatt. Perhaps the most strikingly Louis XIV features are the two doors on the east wall, each surmounted by two tiers of curved pediments: these extraordinary confections were invented by Wyatt in collaboration with Mrs Arbuthnot.[52] Perhaps the closest French parallel is the use of single pediments of this nature, placed above the doors in the Hôtel de Roquelaure (1724–26) by Jean-Baptiste Leroux (*pl. 55*). Scope for wall decoration in the Waterloo Gallery was somewhat limited: Wyatt had to leave as much space as possible for the hanging of pictures, a large portion of which were war booty from the Peninsular Campaigns. Rather than resort to rocaille panelling, he decorated the walls with large Louis XIV picture frames, supplied by Thomas Temple & Son.[53] The large portraits of Queen Mary I, King Charles I and Emperor Rudolph II were set in their heavy Rococo revival frames and placed over curvaceous chimney pieces of Siena marble, originally intended for York House. The west wall of Apsley House was taken up with windows that could be concealed with sliding glass panels. Wyatt aimed to evoke the Galerie des Glaces at Versailles (*pl. 42*), a feature befitting a military hero who had played a crucial part in re-establishing the old order throughout Europe.

Even if Wyatt's reputation was on the wane when he resumed work at Stafford House, his creative abilities remained undimmed: this time he should have had the opportunity to produce State Apartments of unparalleled splendour. However, he was forced to endure the humiliation of a secondary role to a new architect in charge and the frustration that resulted from the vacillations of a duke and duchess who thought they had taste but could never stick to any decision.

The first of these rooms to be completed was the South-West Drawing Room (*pls. 22, 99*). This was the only one with a ceiling painted by a contemporary artist – *The Solar System* by Henry Howard RA (1769–1847; *pl. 108*). Unlike the painted ceilings of the Grands Appartements at Versailles, which would have extended into the coves, Howard's roundel is very much confined to the flat surface of the ceiling. However, far from eschewing seventeenth-century French ornament, Wyatt used scrolls derived from Jean Le Pautre's *Rinceaux des différens feuillages* (*pl. 53*) at the north and south ends of the ceiling, and the cove. He surrounded the painting with a border made up of what he called his "palm and cherry stalk"

Plate 52
Former Green Library, Lancaster
House. This was so named after the
green silk damask wall hangings
supplied by Morel & Seddon in 1829.
It was here that Harriet Beecher Stowe
was received by the Duke and Duchess
of Sutherland on 7 May 1853.

Plate 60
JEAN MARIETTE (1660–1742),
*Décoration de la Chambre de parade de
l'Hôtel d'Evreux du côté de l'estrade ou
[sic] est placé le lict*, engraving from
L'Architecture françoise, Paris 1735–38.
This grouping of columns on pedestals
round the state bed may well have
provided Wyatt with ideas for his
grouping of columns at both ends of
the State Dining Room.

of Jean Cotelle for the ceilings of the State Dining Room or the Ante-Rooms on
the first floor, but he preferred to look elsewhere once the proportions became
elongated. The ceilings at Versailles were either decorated with painted allegories
or, if small enough – as in the case of the Salon d'Œil de Bœuf – largely left
blank. The latter is what Wyatt did on the ground-floor apartments of Stafford
House: the decoration ended at the top of the cove, although sometimes the
dullness of a blank, white ceiling might be mitigated with ornate but rather small
rosettes from which to suspend chandeliers. In the larger State Apartments on the
first floor, he preferred to borrow his designs from Rome or Palmyra rather than
the Ile de France.

In contrast to Wyatt, Barry limited mainly himself to ornament with which
Louis XIV would have been familiar, particularly towards the end of his reign,
and he eschewed the Rococo. Under his covert influence, the Sutherlands made
various requests, particularly in the Picture Gallery, that pushed Wyatt closer
to French Baroque, even if he regarded it as Italian. However, until he finally
resigned, it was Wyatt who made the designs, even though he was often
compelled to study unnamed books of French ornament that travelled back and
forth from Stafford House. This process, combined with the need to assert his

Plate 61
PIERRE LE PAUTRE (*c.* 1648–1716),
untitled interior, engraved by Jean
Mariette, *c.* 1710. A possible source for
Barry's Picture Gallery and State
Dining Room doors, and also Wyatt's
pilasters above the Picture Gallery
picture rail.

architectural authority, may well have made Wyatt examine his engraved sources more closely and at times produce designs more similar to architecture contemporary with Louis XIV than a mere abundance of rocaille.

Posterity's perception of Louis XIV is somewhat coloured by the hackneyed use of this ornament on everyday articles in the years leading up to the Great Exhibition of 1851. Similar views were being aired as early as 1836. George Morant, who carried out much of the decoration of Stafford House, declared at a Parliamentary Select Committee on Arts and Manufactures: "I consider there is a vast deal of bad taste of the style which is called that of Louis XIV."[72] Furthermore, one's prejudices would certainly be confirmed if the use of artificial such materials as Jackson's putty had been put in the hands of lesser craftsmen. However, the surviving interiors of Stafford (now Lancaster) House enable one to see this style in its best light and to understand why Wyatt, even when his career was in decline, was still praised for his excellent taste. At the same hearing, Morant (perhaps expediently) singled out Stafford House as the best example of its sort: "... although it may be in the Louis XIV style, it is done in a way that will produce a striking and a bold effect."[73]

3 *"From my House to your Palace"*

On 14 April 1841 *The Times* reported:

> Stafford House is now nearly finished; the picture gallery is completed. On the 26 May, the Queen's Birthday, the Duke and Duchess will give a dinner of extraordinary magnificence, without distinction of political party, to a numerous and distinguished circle forming the *élite* in high life. Rumour states that the Queen herself will be present.

This brief report very much sets the tone that Stafford House was to maintain until the Sutherlands finally left in 1913. This was the greatest town house of London, where the "*élite* in high life" gathered and royalty often put in an appearance. Once the builders had left, Stafford House took on its palatial air, and was as much associated with grand receptions and troops of servants as it was with its richly gilded interiors.

It should be born in mind that Stafford House occupied its position in the richest city of the richest country in the world, at a time when power and prestige still remained in the hands of the landed interest. Therefore, all manner of distinguished visitors came there: General Garibaldi, Harriet Beecher Stowe, William Gladstone, Frédéric Chopin, Sir Henry Irving, Dr Livingstone, General Botha and the young Winston Churchill, as well as sovereigns and members of royal families at home and abroad. In addition, Stafford House served as a meeting place for a large number of causes, ranging from the Abolition of Slavery to War Relief in the Balkans and South Africa. The building that hosted such gatherings lost none of its splendour during such occupancy: three generations of clerks of works – all from the same family – saw to extensive redecoration when necessary, and to the installation of the latest devices for domestic convenience. At the same time, Stafford House employed the largest and most cosmopolitan staff of servants in London – it even included a Pole and a West Indian – and this served as the engine that kept this vast house going. No visitor could help noticing their presence.

Plate 62
The door leaves of the former Picture Gallery (open) and South-East Ante-Room (closed), Lancaster House. Compare the Louis XIV 'invention' of Benjamin Wyatt's closed doors with the closer attention paid to late French Baroque designs on Charles Barry's open doors. Both were executed by George Jackson & Son.

When Francis Seymour Haden exhibited his basket coffins in the garden of Stafford House in June 1875 (see p. 113), an unknown journalist reported: "the most amusing part of the whole exhibition was to me the faces of the ducal flunkies, who looked on in a sort of quiet despair at this unorthodox intrusion of the outer barbarians on the sacred ground of Staffordhouse [sic]."[1] When Harriet Beecher Stowe visited Stafford House in May 1853, she reported: "what seemed to me an innumerable multitude of servants in livery, with powdered hair, repeated our names through the long corridors, from one to another." They were sufficiently well disciplined for her to comment that they "moved noiselessly to and fro, taking up the various articles on the table, and offering them to the guests in a peculiarly quiet manner".[2]

By 1853 the Stafford House establishment had been functioning smoothly for almost twenty-five years. Indeed, the servants' wages books go back to 1829, when the 1st duke first occupied his new London residence.[3] At that time, there was a household of thirty-eight servants, twenty-two male and sixteen female, headed by Thomas Dodsworth, the steward. Immediately below him were three grooms of the chamber, followed by a butler, under-butler, an usher of the hall, five footmen, a watchman and finally the steward's-room boy, the most junior manservant. The stables establishment was headed by John Jones, the coachman, and below him a second coachman, a postilion and an outrider. Twelve of the fifteen female servants were headed by Mrs Maben, the housekeeper: under her were five housemaids, four laundry maids, a chambermaid, a still-room maid, and a dairymaid. The three kitchen maids worked under Patrick Foley, the cook and the highest-paid servant (103 guineas per annum). The steward was paid 100 guineas a year, the coachman 34 guineas a year, the footmen 24 guineas and the steward's-room boy 14 guineas. The housekeeper's salary was 30 guineas, and the maids' wages ranged from between 18 guineas a year at the most senior level to 10 guineas at the most junior. In addition, the household received yearly board wages, a form of food allowance, ranging from £45. 12s. 6d. for the most senior male servants to £38. 13s. 6d. for the housekeeper and £31. 5s. 8½d. for the maids. When their employer died, the more senior servants could each expect a bonus, worth as much as two years' wages.

The earlier wage books provide glimpses of life in the servants' hall in the days of the 1st duke. Some came from other grand households: Ann Morris, a housemaid taken on in March 1832, was "late with Lady Jersey"; Maria Hainsworth, a still-room maid, had been employed by the Marquis of Lansdowne.[4] A number left to 'better' themselves or get married. Others were dismissed for misdemeanours or inadequacies: in January 1829 Thomas Dance, a footman, left "through improper behaviour to the Groom of the

Chambers at West Hill".[5] Richard Yeo, another footman, was discharged in June 1835 for drunkenness. Mrs Paine, a dairymaid, was dismissed for being "not strong enough" and R. Hemming, a livery helper, for being "too heavy".[6] Quite a few were illiterate: these included Hemming, a number of maids from the Highlands, and a more senior servant such as Edward Ford, who served as the coachman during the 1830s.

By the mid-1830s the wage books were superseded by specially printed forms, listing the posts at Stafford House, Trentham and, after 1849, Cliveden. Furthermore, James Loch had detailed tables drawn up of the Stafford House establishment in April 1844, compared with those of four other noblemen, namely the Dukes of Norfolk and Bedford, the Earl of Carlisle and Lord Francis Egerton.[7] The printed forms indicate that in theory there were about fifty-five servants at or connected with Stafford House, about thirty men, including the stable staff, and about twenty-five women.[8] To the former category belonged the steward, the head of the household and by 1840 the highest-paid servant; below him were the cook, by then the second highest paid; four grooms of chamber, one of whom doubled up as confectioner and another as an upholsterer; an under-butler and second under-butler, the post of butler having been made redundant by about 1840; four footmen, two steward's-room boys, a baker, house carpenter, porter and night porter, as well as a piper – a post created in 1841, when a certain James Macbeth was taken on for that purpose. The stables were maintained by a comptroller, with a staff – in theory, at any rate – of two coachmen, three postillions and three grooms, though the numbers could swell to as many as fifteen.

The housekeeper might have up to eight women under her: a still-room maid, confectioners' maid and plate woman, as well as five housemaids. The laundry, which by the 1840s was outside her jurisdiction, was staffed by the duchess's laundress and as many as six laundry maids. The cook had up to four kitchen maids and a baker working under him full-time. The servants "upstairs" were employed either as personal maids to the duchess and her elder daughters (viz. the duchess's dressmaker, duchess's maid and young ladies' maid) or in the nursery, where there were, in theory, posts for three nurses and two nursemaids. In practice, the staff seldom reached its full complement: granted, there would usually be the full complement of five housemaids, but after about 1840 there was no butler; and usually only three out of four footmen or kitchen maids. By 1850 the post of duchess's laundress had been dispensed with.

All households have their own rules, but those of Stafford House remain as yet untraced. In 1830 Thomas Dodsworth issued a *Memorandum as to Servants*, which in fact only concerned the footmen. The first had to be dressed by nine o'clock, attend to the bells and blinds in the lower apartments, and not quit the hall unless sent for. The second was to be dressed by half past eleven, attend to the blinds regularly and walk with Lady Stafford when required. He was also to "take charge of the dinner" and see that all the plates were washed up "by getting up". The third was to deliver messages and go out with the carriage when required.[9] When the 2nd Duke of Sutherland inherited his father's title and estates, he felt that standards had lapsed and that he should spell it out that all staff should obey the steward's rules or face dismissal.[10] The Italian mannerisms of L. Vantini, the new steward, may well have invited ridicule from the servants, who were more used to an Englishman such as Thomas Dodsworth, his predecessor. Servants did from time to time misbehave in other properties: on one occasion duchess Harriet dismissed a footman for getting a housemaid pregnant after making love in a churchyard near Trentham. However, both the relative silence on the subject of servants' discipline and the impressions created on outsiders indicate that Stafford House ran smoothly: it was the costs that caused anxiety.

Even if no comprehensive list of servants' duties has survived, some posts, such as cook, nurse or laundry maid, would seem fairly self-explanatory. More obscure-sounding posts, such as still-room maid or groom of chambers, might require explanation. In most cases, different servants' duties are laid down in *The Complete Servant*, compiled by Samuel and Sarah Adams (London 1825); and it is reasonable to assume that they would have differed little at Stafford House. The housekeeper controlled the female servants, and had care of the household furniture and linen: Harriet Galleazzi was largely responsible for compiling the 1839 inventory.[11] The still-room maid had responsibility for the stores. In addition, there were housemaids, whose jobs were probably the most arduous. Expected to be up and about by five o'clock in the morning, their work ranged from making beds, opening shutters and lighting fires to all manner of cleaning, from curtains, furniture and grates to marble. The lady's maid was a senior female servant who would have been at her mistress's beck and call but independent of the housekeeper. It would have been her task to help dress her mistress, do her hair, supervise her wardrobe, and clean and repair clothes as necessary. These she could often claim as a perquisite, once her mistress no longer wanted them.

Of all the servants, male and female, the house steward was the most important: he was grand enough to have his own servant, the steward's-room boy. Second in the hierarchy were a series of grooms of chambers, whose job was to attend to visiting professionals and tradesmen. For example, Michael Gummow supervised the architects who measured up the work done for the Duke of York at Stafford House;[12] and George London inadvertently allowed Desiré Dellier, the rogue upholsterer, to remove chairs that he then tried to pass on to his creditors.[13]

Plate 63

JOHN PARTRIDGE (1790–1872), *George Granville, 2nd Duke of Sutherland*, c. 1850, oil on canvas, Sutherland, Dunrobin Castle, Sutherland Trust. This painting was probably executed late in the duke's life. The State Apartments, with a bronze statue of his eldest son by J.-J. Feuchère, can be seen in the background.

A Stafford House groom of chamber usually doubled up as an upholsterer or valet, whose job was to carry out the equivalent duties for his master that the lady's maid did for her mistress. Below them was the under-butler, who would have been responsible for cleaning plate, china and glass, and setting out the sideboard. His subordinates, the footmen, would have laid the cutlery and waited at table. In most households, and no doubt Stafford House as well, the footmen were supposed to open doors and answer the bell, to brush clothes and clean more delicate pieces of furniture, such as gilt mirrors and frames. The hall porter's domain was the Entrance Hall, and his duties would have been to answer the door and take in all messages, parcels and letters. The livery of the male servants, very much regarded as a perk, consisted of a light "drab" dress coat and gaiters, with silver and scarlet epaulettes, silver lace garters and scarlet breeches.[14]

Ordinary servants' wages stayed much the same between the late 1820s and the 1840s. Board wages were permitted only to the laundry maids: Ebenezer Thurgood, the teetotal baker, requested them in place of what he called "drinking wages", so that he could eat his meals in his own apartment and avoid being the "butt of insult and object of scorn" to the other servants.[15] The duchess turned down the plea, but five years later (1849) suggested reintroducing board wages in order to save money: the idea found little favour with James Loch, and was never implemented.[16] Although no higher than the other great households of that time, the consumption of meat was substantial: it was calculated in 1844 at an average of 1 lb 9 oz. per person a day; a modest figure, however, when compared with that of Lord Zetland's household – 2lb 8oz.[17] In addition, male servants were allowed a beer allowance of one small quart a day, and the female servants a pint.[18] During the Highland famines of the late 1840s, Walker decided to set an example by limiting the consumption of poultry, then comparatively expensive, to the duke's table.[19] As a result of Thurgood's one-man temperance campaign, combined with the desire to save money wherever possible, the strength of the beer was reduced, much to the annoyance of the servants. As a substitute for drink during leisure hours, the servants were encouraged to borrow books from a servants' library, organized by Thomas Jackson, the duke's private secretary. In spite of their (understandable) irritation with Thurgood, the household were praised by Walker: "a more steady & moral set of servants I never saw."[20]

As one would expect, the servants were mostly either English or Scots. The most conspicuous of the latter were the pipers, who played at banquets and often served as valets. The most famous of all was John MacAlister, the 3rd duke's piper, who made his début at the court of Tsar Alexander II in 1856, to the consternation of the officers but delight of Grand Duchess Constantine.[21] The chefs were mostly

French: M. Raybond, who prepared luncheon for Harriet Beecher Stowe, confirmed her impression that the "*cuisine* of these west end regions appears to be entirely under French legislation": apparently, he bore "the reputation of being the first artist of his class in England".[22] In addition, there were French laundry maids such as Mme Rousseau, and French nursery maids such as Claudine Chapuis and Eulalie Crépin. The German contingent included non-servants such as Dr Bernard Gäbler, the tutor (see below), and Countess Dembriska, the governess from Hamburg, referred to by Duchess Harriet as "the little Countess".[23] Besides them there were at least two German (or possibly Swiss) young ladies' maids, Mlle Friedel and Mme Ritz. One groom of chambers, by the name of Francis Poponski, came from Poland. In spite of her Italian married name, Mrs Galleazzi, the longest-serving housekeeper (1838–54), was in fact born in Middlesex.[24] Only one black servant is recorded as working at Stafford House – an unfortunate valet, by the name of Charlie Stair, whom the 3rd duke brought home from St Kitts after a yachting trip to the West Indies.[25] After the duke's death, Stair was kept on by the Dowager Duchess Mary Caroline, only to be dismissed in 1894 for getting drunk on champagne at a servant's wedding.[26]

From the late 1850s the household hovered at about forty servants. Their wages remained much the same, but by 1859 Mrs Lee, the new housekeeper, was being paid 50 guineas a year, ten more than Mrs Galleazi had been by 1851.[27] During the late 1870s the kitchen staff increased to a point where there were two French chefs, an English steward's-room cook and two extra still-room maids.[28] M. Detraz, the head chef, was earning £200, the same as Whittaker, the steward, and Mrs Low, the housekeeper, got 60 guineas. In 1889 the 3rd duke (*pl. 65*) married his mistress, Mary Caroline Blair (*pl. 100*), within months of his first wife's death. Following the resulting rupture with his family and ostracism by society, the duke led a more reclusive existence. The surviving meal book of the period lists dinners of no more than five people. Furthermore, Duchess Mary Caroline set about drastic economies and sacked large numbers of servants: she is alleged to have pocketed the savings.[29]

After the death of the 3rd duke in 1892, almost all the remaining servants were dismissed. Although against "turning people out abruptly", Duchess Millicent (*pl. 74*) wanted "to put fresh women into Stafford House" – no doubt in order to clear it of any associations with her hated stepmother-in-law.[30] Although the overall picture becomes fainter after about 1890 – almost all the household accounts relevant to Stafford House have disappeared – there were probably about thirty servants left. In the latter decades of the nineteenth century, there were usually as many female as male servants, and the 1913 *Men Servants Tax* return lists five permanently stationed at Stafford House and nine "travelling servants".[31]

Plate 64
Ceiling and west wall of the former
State Dining Room or Banqueting
Room, now known as the Music Room,
Lancaster House. This dining room
was completed by the end of 1840.
Barry was responsible for details such
as the door panels, insets and surface
recesses of the archway. The
remainder, including the monumental
ceiling, is the work of Benjamin Wyatt.

The household was run by the steward. As well as the managing of the servants, he was also responsible for the household accounts. He was meant to keep strict hours, and was not allowed to smoke in his office, take perquisites or accept commissions from tradesmen.[32] Perhaps the two most prominent personalities were L. Vantini and his successor, Richard Walker. Steward from 1833 until 1840, Vantini spiritedly struggled with the English language, with occasionally hilarious results: on one occasion he referred to the 1st duke as "the late Duck", and on another he entered Sherburn & Sam's Italian Warehouse in the account books as "Italian Whorehouse".[33] His strong Italian accent, so evident even in his letters, could all too easily have given rise to the ridicule that prompted the duke to reinforce discipline "below stairs". Vantini's method of accounting, based on recording receipts sent in by tradesmen rather than payments as he made them, particularly exasperated Thomas Jackson, the duke's private secretary. Their relationship was stormy: on one occasion, Vantini demanded a formal hearing of all his grievances against Jackson in front of the duke, duchess and entire household. Nevertheless, even if his methods were frequently called into question, Jackson was prepared to concede that the actual accounts were "substantially correct".[34] Vantini eventually left in November 1840 to become manager of the Euston and Victoria Station hotels,[35] and was later to help found the Northern Church of England School.[36]

Vantini was succeeded by Richard Walker, probably the best steward in the eyes of his employers. As well as having to enforce unpopular measures, such as the weakening of the servants' beer, he was regarded as an excellent accountant. Thomas Jackson was to write: "his method of keeping his cash account is so clear he can always tell at any moment what his balance is."[37] On James Loch's instructions, Walker drew up a table comparing the Sutherlands's household expenses with those of his cousins, the Dukes of Bedford and Norfolk, the Earl of Carlisle and Lord Francis Egerton. Loch used this information to reassure the duke that he never spent more than they did on individual articles.[38] Nevertheless, his annual wage bill, amounting to £2685, remained considerably higher: the closest figure, that of the Duke of Bedford, was nearer £1500.[39] Despairing over mounting costs, the duchess suspected Walker of "mismanagement".[40] The latter, aware of her extravagant nature, diplomatically suggested that she should be made aware of the cost of articles before she bought them.[41] Nevertheless, when he had to retire in 1853 because of ill health, Loch praised his keeping the establishment "in excellent order",[42] and the duchess thought fit to grant him a pension of £50 per annum, "strictly as a matter of regard during well performed thirteen years of Service".[43]

George Loch, who succeeded his father as agent in 1855, concerned himself with far fewer household details than his father had. So long as stewards kept both

their staff and accounts in order, he was not troubled. However, in August 1875 a Mr Bliss was promptly sacked for running up an overdraft with Messrs Drummonds of over £1000 on the household account.[44] His replacement by John Whittaker in September 1875 was none too amicable: the latter was determined not to overlap with his predecessor "longer than is absolutely necessary".[45] In contrast, Whittaker was sufficiently competent to last beyond the death of the 3rd duke in 1892. He was replaced in October 1893: no specific reason was recorded, but presumably the 4th duke wanted a new steward with no misplaced loyalty towards the hated dowager duchess. With the demise of John Culverwell, the duke's agent, in 1900, the Loch method of committing domestic details to paper died out. Compared with his earlier predecessors, J. Sim, the last steward of Stafford House, seems little more than a name on a tax return. Eighty years earlier, he would have corresponded actively with the agent on all manner of household concerns. In the closing years, it was probably felt that domestic matters could easily be settled over the telephone and no longer demanded copious correspondence.

When one considers all the splendour of Stafford House, it is easy to forget that it housed a family and that children were brought up there. Those depicted by J. Digman Wingfield (*pls. 82–84*) playing on the floor of the Picture Gallery might seem somewhat incongruous amid the old masters and gilding, but they formed a vitally important part of life at Stafford House. But what was it like to be a child at Stafford House? To answer the question, we must turn to the remarkably precocious diaries kept by Lord Ronald Gower from his childhood onwards. Lord Ronald (*pl. 66*), the youngest son of the 2nd Duke of Sutherland, was born in 1845. His mother's favourite child, he inherited his father's love for the arts and was to prove himself a fine sculptor and distinguished art historian. He was an Antiquary, Trustee of the National Portrait Gallery and referred to himself as plain 'Gower' as opposed to Leveson-Gower. A confirmed bachelor, he is meant to have served as a model for Lord Henry Wotton in Oscar Wilde's *The Picture of Dorian Gray*. In his old age he lost almost all his money, and died in 1916 with little left but an abundance of wistfully nostalgic memories of the great London house that his family no longer possessed.

Being one of the richest families in Britain, the Sutherlands could afford to spare no cost in educating their children, although it must be said that the 3rd duke's tutor, the Revd G.H. Bunsen, was seen as amiable but rather ineffectual and the "most constant billiard player".[46] The Leveson-Gower daughters were taught by "the little Countess" Dembriska from Hamburg.[47] So were the boys, until they were old enough for Dr Gäbler. Lord Ronald Gower fondly

Plate 66

Lord Ronald Gower (1845–1916). Although born Lord Ronald Leveson-Gower, he preferred to omit the 'Leveson'. A distinguished art historian and fine amateur sculptor, Lord Ronald Gower FSA, the youngest surviving child of the 2nd Duke of Sutherland, served as the family chronicler. He also reputedly served as the model for Lord Henry Wotton in Oscar Wilde's *The Picture of Dorian Gray*, but, unlike Wilde, he stopped short of legal action and temporarily fled the country when involved in a homosexual scandal.

remembered her, and even paid her a visit in Paris at the height of the Franco-Prussian War. By then an old lady, she still cut a spirited figure who "breathed fire and slaughter against the Emperor and his Government" and who did not seem "at all alarmed at the prospect of a bombardment, or occupation of Paris".[48] One might assume that in the more sedate surroundings of Stafford House, she would have taught the girls and her sisters French and probably German (young Lord Ronald could write basic German at an early age). Gabrielle Rossetti, father of the painter Dante Gabriel Rossetti, taught them Italian.[49] In addition, Lady Constance had seven guineas' worth of piano lessons from Frédéric Chopin.[50] Once their education had ended, they fulfilled their mother's hopes that they should 'marry well': Lady Elizabeth became Duchess of Argyll, Lady Caroline Duchess of Leinster, Lady Constance Duchess of Westminster, and Lady Evelyn, the eldest, married Lord Blantyre.

Unlike his sisters, Lord Ronald Gower kept a journal from the age of nine. His tutor was Bernard Gäbler, a philologist from Saxe-Altenberg, who organized his daily routine, which he recorded in his entry for 28 January 1855:[51]

All as usual, I shall write down our plan for lessons *during* the day.

7–8. Preparation of Latin, Greek, German or French./ *8–9*. Breakfast and Prayers/ *9–10*. Latin or Arithmetic./ *10–11*. Greek or Drawing,/ *11–12*. Lunch, and Reading or Drawing./ *12–1*. Walk or Music or Drill./ *1–2*. Latin or Reading./ *2–3*. Dinner./ *3–4*. Walk or Ride./ *4–5*. History or Geography./ *5–6*. German or French./ *6–7*. Tea and Private Journal./ *7*. Reading and hymns. Sometimes we go to bed at ½ past 8 and sometimes later. *Mr Ogg* is our Latin and English Master.

Mr Masters is our Music Master. *Mr Kenworthy* our Drawing Master, *Serjeant Major Hockey* or [*sic*] drilling Master.

Gäbler had published a learned work in German on the Thirty-Nine Articles,[52] then regarded as the backbone of the Anglican faith, but he was not above sending his charge a valentine card.[53] Lord Ronald often went with his mother to exhibitions at Marlborough House or the British Museum. On one occasion, he went with her to watch a performance by the Christie Minstrels: so impressed was the duchess that she invited them to sing for the Duchess of Cambridge at Stafford House on 17 March 1855. According to Lord Ronald, "they sang in the hall, a platform was erected against the 2 columns they sang very well ..." His parents realized his early propensity for collecting *objets d'art*: not only did he buy medallions and shells, but when he had two teeth pulled out, he was rewarded for his bravery with an antique bronze from his father.[54] Nevertheless, Lord Ronald's childhood seems to have been happy and indulged, nothing like as rigidly disciplined as those of his contemporaries in the Royal Family. In an age when children were meant to be seen and not heard, he would seem to have been remarkably close to his parents, and he wrote fondly of them. Just after his father had died at Trentham, his words, as an adolescent, were: "one can hardly believe it possible that one will never hear his kind voice or see him here again."[55]

For Lord Ronald's great-nephew, the 5th Duke of Sutherland, Stafford House was probably the least favourite of his father's residences. His memories are of tedious lessons (he had a particular aversion towards mathematics), mitigated by pantomimes, pageants and giving his mother or nanny the slip in Green Park whenever the opportunity arose.[56] Judging from the 5th duke's reminiscences and Lord Ronald Gower's journals, Stafford House would have been very much associated with lessons, governesses and tutors, while Dunrobin and Trentham would have meant fresh air and outdoor pursuits.

Births and deaths occurred at Stafford House. In the first week of August 1845, not only Duchess Harriet but also her daughters Evelyn, Lady Blantyre and Elizabeth, Lady Lorne (later Duchess of Argyll) gave birth there, earning it the nickname "the lying-in hospital".[57] However, a letter written by Duchess Harriet to her husband just before her confinement gave instructions as to her burial and the bringing up of the younger children, should she die in childbirth. She specifically asked to be buried at Trentham, "near the Infants we have lost – and I hope that when God wills you away – your dear remains may rest by mine".[58] In the event, she did not die until 1868, some four years after her husband, with Lord Ronald at her bedside: unlike her daughter-in-law, Duchess Annie, at least she did not die a wronged wife (see chapter 5). This particular deathbed scene, which would occur some twenty years later, Lord Ronald recounted with all pathos:

When I went up to her bedside & kissed her hand she said – poor darling – referring to my beloved mother's death – "It's so soon; and in the same room!". She suffered much but bore up with marvellous courage…she said "Cannot you give me cloroform [*sic*] – No it would not be right". But she said it had been given to my mother; which was the case, & she showed how clear her mind was. Mr Hewett [a clergyman] knelt at the foot of the bed and said some prayers…When he asked if she wished him to pray she said "Yes – The Commendatory prayer" – and she added, "read it in a loud voice"…just before midnight as we knelt with her, after a very deeply drawn breath the end came, and her soul, I trust & feel certain – entered into the everlasting Peace.[59]

Soon after Duchess Annie's death, Queen Victoria visited Stafford House and recorded, perhaps with more restraint, in her diary for 27 November 1888:

there she lay, looking very pretty, peaceful & young again, with her hands

Plate 67
East wall and door of the former State Dining Room, Lancaster House. The doors and insets are very much in the style of Pierre Le Pautre, and were made by George Jackson to Charles Barry's designs. The columns are the work of Benjamin Wyatt.

folded, & a smile on her face, as if she were going to speak, – covered with white flowers, In that same room my dear former Duchess died. The Beautiful staircase & house, all covered up. looked very gloomy.[60]
This is the last time Queen Victoria is known to have visited Stafford House.

A house of the size and importance of Stafford House needed constant maintenance: for this purpose the Sutherlands retained John Fish as the clerk of works on a salary of £250 once the building had been completed. After his death in 1859, the position was held by his son, John Fish the younger, and from about 1890 by his grandson, Percy Fish. After 1842 no significant alteration to the building took place. Once Barry had finished his work, there was no further use for architects. Any further improvements or redecoration were left in the hands of the Fish family.

In earlier days, John Fish often found himself in the unenviable position of being servant to two masters, in the form of Robert Smirke and Benjamin Wyatt, who were frequently in conflict. Once Charles Barry had finished, Fish's job was to supervise builders' work and to stay at Stafford House when the Sutherlands were absent. Among other things, he supervised the repainting and regilding of the dome of the Principal Staircase in 1852.[61] As the Sutherlands became increasingly conscious of rising expenses, they felt that competent as Fish was, his salary of £250 per annum was not justified by the amount of work that he did. He successfully resisted any attempts to assign him responsibility for Trentham, but he was made to supervise works at Cliveden. When the newly acquired house was burnt down, Fish was absent and could not be found at Stafford House. As a result, he incurred the lasting displeasure of his employers.[62] Nevertheless, although prone to ill health, Fish was kept on for another ten years, until he died a few days after falling from scaffolding on the portico of Stafford House in October 1859.[63] The duke attended his funeral at Brompton Cemetery, paying all expenses, but wishing "no ostentatious display".[64] Ten years earlier, in the aftermath of the fire at Cliveden, the duchess had raged against Fish's negligence. On his death, she wrote with a modicum of affection: "I can hardly think we are not to see him across the stairs."[65]

John Fish the younger, who had recently been appointed clerk of works to Lord Ellesmere at Bridgewater House, was asked to take over at Cliveden in April 1860.[66] His involvement with Stafford House seems to have begun largely as a result of the Empress Eugénie's visit in December 1860 and her (unfulfilled) determination to have a similar residence built for herself. Although he could find no complete set of Wyatt's drawings, he managed to unearth a sufficient number "to compile and trace the principal parts of all the work done ... as to the ornament & finish of the State Rooms". The walls and furniture of the house were

uncovered, at Fish's suggestion, so that photographs (untraced) could be taken. He argued: "the Empress saw the house in its perfection with all its wealth of furniture, ornaments, draperies, sculpture & pictures and it seemed to me that successful photographs would be a most suitable and handsome way of conveying the due effect of the rooms."[67]

As his duties were comparatively light, John Fish the younger worked for only £50 a year until July 1875, when his salary was substantially increased as a result of six years' heavy work and expenditure on the drains.[68] The problem recurred throughout the 1870s: when Sir Henry Cole visited Stafford House in May 1878, Lord Stafford, the duke's eldest son, "complained of the Stinks in his bed room".[69] Flooding occurred in the basement in 1878 and in the kitchen offices in July 1880. Fish remedied the situation by making improvements at the point where the drain entered the main sewer.[70] Drains were not Fish's only preoccupation. He saw to the replacing of incompetent or ageing staff in his province,[71] the installation of lifts in 1882,[72] and the cleaning and repairing of the gilding in the Picture Gallery in 1890.[73] Successful experiments had been conducted to install electricity in the Picture Gallery in 1882, and it was permanently installed in most of the State Apartments, excluding the Banqueting Room, by 1891.[74] By August

1892 John Fish the younger had been replaced by his son Percy. The latter was kept on by the 4th duke, and his main task was to complete the installation of electricity throughout the house and supervise extensive redecoration (sadly, the relevant bills are lost) at a cost of £42,850, carried out by Messrs Trollope and the Decorative Arts Guild,[75] all in time for Bedford Lemère to photograph the interiors in July 1895.[76] No further works of this nature are recorded at Stafford House: Percy Fish had almost certainly left by 1913,[77] and as far as we know, he was the last of the line of a family that for three generations had ensured that the building remained in good repair.

What role did Stafford House play in a wider context? It could be described as the ballroom of London, but in no way as a political nerve centre until the 1900s. Before then, the Sutherlands had been more prominent at court. Both Duchess Harriet and Duchess Annie served as Mistresses of the Robes: the queen's refusal to part with the former when Sir Robert Peel became Prime Minister in 1841 created a constitutional crisis. It is true that all four dukes had, in early adulthood, been Whig and later Liberal Members of Parliament; Duchess Annie was a member of the Primrose League; and Joseph Chamberlain appointed the 4th duke President of the Tariff Reform League in 1908. But after the 1st duke, none had held a ministry, nor did they make many speeches in the House of Lords. It was in court rather than political circles that they moved. The Prince Consort became godfather to Lord Albert Leveson-Gower in 1844, and the queen godmother to two daughters of the 2nd duke in 1841 and 1848 respectively, and to one daughter of the 4th duke (then Lord Stafford) in 1885 (all three died in infancy). Nevertheless, the queen and Prince Consort, and later the Prince and Princess of Wales, frequently visited Stafford House, and remained on close and friendly terms with the Sutherlands.

With its huge staircase, banqueting rooms and Picture Gallery, Stafford House entertained more heads of state, politicians and celebrities than any other private house in London. As early as June 1830 the 1st duke had entertained Prince Friedrich Wilhelm of Prussia.[78] From the early 1840s sovereigns, princes and statesmen went through the specially constructed glass doors and mounted the Principal Staircase to the State Apartments. For much of the nineteenth century it was associated with enlightened causes, such as two Concerts for the Polish Refugees, at one of which Liszt played on 5 June 1841; *The memorial from the women of England to the women of the United States on the subject of slavery* (1852); and visits from Harriet Beecher Stowe (1853) and Giuseppe Garibaldi (1864), the two most celebrated and best-recorded guests of the nineteenth century.

On 26 November 1852 the *grandes dames* of Whig society met at Stafford

Plate 69
View of the Great Hall and Principal
Staircase, photographed from the
north-west by Bedford Lemère,
Stafford House, 1895. *Erin* by Baron
Marochetti stands on the landing, and
G.C. Cali's *Luna* can just be seen
tucked under the staircase.

House to address their memorial to the women of America on slavery, and
organize the gathering of signatures. Although they denied any political or
nationalist motives, the wife of the former President John Tyler sent an irate letter
to *The Times* (15 February 1853), in which she challenged the duchess to look closer
to home: in her view, the poor of Britain were far worse off than slaves on the
Southern plantations. Harriet Beecher Stowe's novel *Uncle Tom's Cabin* struck an
emotional chord with Englishwomen, both elevated and humble. The *grandes
dames* flocked to Stafford House to hear Mrs M.E. Webb, "a lady of colour", give
recitations from this work.[79] By March 1853, what *The Times* called the "Uncle Tom
anti-slavery movement"[80] had amassed some 562,848 signatures, which were
displayed with the original declaration in the Caledonian Hotel, off the Strand.

Indeed, the author herself recorded her visit to Stafford House in *Sunny
Memories of Foreign Lands*. The first person she met was Donald Mackenzie, by
now the Sutherlands' piper. Proceeding with "only a confused idea of passing from
passage to passage and from hall to hall", she reached what she thought was a
"large drawing room" (in fact the Green Library), filled with an abundance of

"works of virtu", all arranged "without any eye to unity of impression". She found the duchess full of "warm and simple kindness" and the duke "with an air of gentleness and dignity", but somewhat withdrawn from society, owing to the "delicacy of his health". It is clear that they ate in the Lower Dining Room: the Duke of Sutherland led her by the arm from the Green Library "through a suite of rooms". After luncheon, which included a course in the form of "a plover's nest, with five little blue specked eggs in it", they "ascended to the picture gallery, passing … the grand staircase and hall". When all were assembled in the Picture Gallery, Lord Shaftesbury delivered a "very short, kind and considerate" speech of welcome, to which – much to her relief – she was not obliged to reply. The company then dispersed to admire the Ante-Rooms, which Mrs Stowe thought had "no unity of impression" – like the Green Library. Nevertheless, being entertained in such opulent surroundings and lionized by such 'enlightened' company as Lord Macaulay and William Gladstone, not to mention a gathering of Whig ladies, left Mrs Stowe deeply gratified with the attitude of the "women of England".

Perhaps the most important visit paid to Stafford House during the nineteenth century was that of Giuseppe Garibaldi in April 1864 (*pl. 71*). The Italian general visited Great Britain to express his gratitude to English supporters for the aid they had given him during his Sicilian campaigns in 1860 and to receive medical attention for a wound that he had sustained at Aspromonte during the previous year. So tumultuous was his welcome in London that the body of his carriage had been wrenched from its chassis by the time of his arrival, and the portals of Stafford House barely kept out the mob. Meanwhile, Garibaldi's sons were lodged in a cheap hotel, and radical elements resented the idea of their hero staying with a duke for fourteen days. It would seem that the Corporation of London asked the duke to play host: he was to make a speech acknowledging their thanks soon after Garibaldi left.[81] He was following in the tradition of his parents, who had held a luncheon in honour of the Neapolitan exiles in April 1858[82] and a concert in May 1859.[83] Although she was now dowager duchess and had been renting Chiswick House from the Duke of Devonshire since 1862, Harriet very much took precedence over her daughter-in-law on this occasion: she laid on such artists as George Watts to paint Garibaldi's portrait, for which he sat between visits from various working men's delegations; she gave him and the London fire brigade, which had turned up to parade in his honour, a tour of the Picture Gallery ('Staff', as the 3rd duke was known, was a keen fireman); she made him sit for two hours reciting Italian poetry to her; and, on the night of the great banquet of 13 April, she even encouraged the general – much to her family's surprise – to smoke in her sitting room, a habit abhorred by her late husband but freely indulged in by

Plate 70
Garibaldi's slipper. Whether given to Duchess Harriet or left behind is not known.

106   LANCASTER HOUSE

the Picture Gallery on 30 June 1882 in aid of this institute.[109] Following a successful experiment a fortnight earlier, the event was lit by the newfangled electric light.

In the tradition of Duchess Harriet's "Uncle Tom Committees", the duke and duchess hosted a meeting at Stafford House on the East African slave trade question in May 1874.[110] Among those who spoke was the American journalist Henry Stanley, famed for his encounter with Dr Livingstone. However, his proposals to establish naval patrols and a court of law staffed by Europeans in order to stamp out the traffic found little support with Benjamin Disraeli. Such measures, in his view, would only antagonize the Sultan of Zanzibar, who had broken no treaty and on whose co-operation existing arrangements depended.

In addition to charity events, Stafford House hosted charity committee meetings such as the famous Stafford House Committees, first on behalf of "The Relief of Suffering among the Turkish Soldiers", and secondly on behalf of "The Sick and Wounded in South Africa". Following the invasion of Turkish soil by the Russians in 1876, the Duke of Sutherland – with an eye, one suspects, to gaining contracts to build railways in the Ottoman Empire – established a committee to supply Turkish troops with warm clothing and their hospitals with drugs and equipment. Lord Blantyre, the duke's brother-in-law, gave just over £3355, and the Duke of Portland £6000. A total of just over £43,750 was raised, and some fifty-three surgeons sent out. This act of philanthropy – only a year after Gladstone had denounced the 'Bashi-Bazouks' and their atrocities in Bulgaria – had its critics. *The Echo* (28 December 1876) observed the absence of "any duke opposite a thumping sum", when the Bulgars were suffering. A more patriotic cause, but one conducted on a far smaller scale, was the relief of the troops in the South African Wars. The duke's raising of money to supply the British Army with a surgeon-general and six trained nurses attracted the support of the Duchess of Teck, the Grand Duchess of Mecklenburg-Strelitz and Lady Burdett-Coutts. The presence of this medical team in South Africa was much appreciated by Sir Garnet Wolseley, the commander-in-chief, but criticized by *The World* (11 June 1879), which questioned the wisdom of entrusting the welfare of the troops to a "representative body of fashionable dames". Entertaining Garibaldi, drumming up support for South African relief and being a zealous fireman greatly enhanced Staff's somewhat populist image, but his attempts to aid Turkish soldiers, as the duke himself admitted, provoked much hostility.

Staff sustained a boundless enthusiasm for technology, inventions and business. London was the centre of world commerce, and at Stafford House the duke chaired meetings in support of his many short-lived schemes, ranging from a "staggering" attempt to persuade the British government to purchase all the railways in Egypt,[111] to forming the Asia Minor and Euphrates Railway Company in 1878 in order to build a railway between Constantinople and the Persian Gulf, thus facilitating trade with India.[112] On this occasion, too, the British government showed no interest and the scheme died a death. Nearer home, there was the launching of Scott's Sewage Company, actively advocated by Sir Henry Cole, among other things an enthusiastic if not always successful entrepreneur. Both he and Major-General Henry Scott persuaded the duke to become chairman of this company in 1872, the purpose of which was to convert sewage partly into manure and partly into cheap cement. Cole appealed to the duke's sense of *noblesse oblige* by telling him that he would be "King of Cleanliness for the Country" if he took part in this scheme.[113] When the Bank of England refused to lend on guarantee, the duke was cajoled by Cole into taking on that onerous role himself – "as a Duke ... *he* must be the Sole guarantor".[114] Nevertheless, the company did not prosper, and after the last meeting at Stafford House, on 30 March 1882, the duke's involvement with this enterprise ended.

Staff's enthusiasm for innovations extended itself to the Earth to Earth Society, a movement founded by Francis Seymour Haden. At a time when towns were expanding on an unprecedented scale and graveyards filling up, Haden advocated the use of perishable coffins, as opposed to the airtight and virtually indestructible ones in use at the time, in order to facilitate the decomposing of bodies and the speedy re-use of graves. Twenty coffins, some made of wicker, some of bark and moss, were laid out along the terrace of Stafford House for the general public to see. This was probably the first time that such a large number of people had been allowed into the grounds. The journalist who had remarked on the "quiet despair" of the "ducal flunkies" (see p. 86) was amused to observe two ladies contemplating an open basketwork coffin and saying that "it would be so nice and cool in the summer".[115] The humour associated with the coolness of the coffins was echoed in *Punch*, wherein they were described as "awfully nice and deliciously cool".[116]

To at least one journalist present, the opening of the grounds of Stafford House for the coffin display might have been regarded as one of the first signs of democracy seeping into the great town house of St James's. A somewhat populist gesture – the only one known to have been carried out by Duchess Mary Caroline – was to throw open Stafford House to some six hundred shop girls (*The Star*, 23 June 1891). The duchess, known for "the liveliest interest in the welfare of the working classes", received them "with simple cordiality and friendliness", and after they were shown through the State Apartments, they were treated to a concert of sacred music under the direction of Signor Carlo Ducci. At the end of the article the wish was expressed that "great houses containing historic and national treasures might occasionally be thrown open for the delight and instruction of the people on Sunday afternoon". Duchess Mary Caroline had started a process that the 4th duke and Duchess Millicent were to pursue for the final two decades of occupancy. The latter's huge charity events and trade fairs made it possible for anyone to visit the house during such an event.

Between 1892 and 1912 the social gatherings at Stafford House were presided over by Duchess Millicent, the beautiful and brilliant hostess, at whose parties "you met or saw … every one you ever heard of or hoped to meet".[117] The "quiet and unostentatious manner"[118] of 'Strath', the 4th duke (*pl. 75*), provided a good foil to his charismatic wife. Duchess Millicent enjoyed the company of artists, poets and 'Souls', and gave Friday-evening soirées for such people.[119] On one such occasion, she even fell victim to a practical joke at the hands of an actor who posed as Father Gapon, the Russian radical.[120] Known as "Meddlesome Millie" and mildly ridiculed as "Interfering Iris, the Countess of Chell" by Arnold Bennet in *The Card*,[121] Duchess Millicent had a sincere wish to do good: she campaigned against the use of lead glazing in the pottery industry, and devoted herself to charitable causes such as the Potteries Cripples' Guild, and the Scottish Home

Plate 74
JOHN SINGER SARGENT RA
(1856–1925), *Millicent, Duchess of
Sutherland* [1867–1955], charcoal on
paper, drawn and exhibited at the
Royal Academy, London, 1905,
Sutherland, Dunrobin Castle,
Sutherland Trust. A keen
philanthropist, widely known as
"Meddlesome Millie", Duchess
Millicent was also perhaps the most
glamorous society hostess in the years
leading up to the First World War.

Industries Association. Every summer she sold the products of both organizations in the gardens of Stafford House. Her more Liberal sympathies had lead her to entertain Boer generals, "dressed in very provincial evening suits",[122] amid the glitter of Stafford House in 1902. Nevertheless, during the 1890s, it was in the field of commerce that she chose to show her patriotism and philanthropy.

In May 1894 she lent the Picture Gallery for the National Silk Textile Exhibition, and from 1906 Duchess Millicent held an annual fair in the gardens of Stafford House for the Scottish Home Industries and Potteries Cripples' Guild. Tweeds,

carpets and rugs were sold, as were artificial flowers, basketwork, and hand-wrought metal objects. When Edward VII visited the display in 1909, selected items were exhibited in the Picture Gallery. Initially, the girls of D.H. Evans manned the stalls, but by 1907 they were helped out by the Duchesses of Wellington and Roxburgh and the Countess of Mar and Kellie. By 1910, a year in which grey and heather-coloured Highland tweeds were the height of fashion, the stalls that sold such items seem to have been exclusively manned by *grandes dames*. The final fair, set for 30 June 1913, had to be cancelled, as Strath became seriously ill with pleurisy that month and died at Dunrobin Castle three days beforehand.

Charitable concerts and fêtes were given in aid of various good causes: perhaps the most spectacular was the Lifeboat Fête, held on 26 June 1901. For a mere two guineas, the visitor would be "free to wander through the magnificent rooms and galleries and corridors, free to examine at leisure the pictures ... as free as it were a private reception and be an honoured guest".[123] The performers included Dame Nellie Melba, and Mr Ben Greet's company staged *The Comedy of Errors* in the garden. On the actual night, it was reported that fewer people turned up than expected. Nevertheless, it had "attracted the man in the street and those who had a fancy to see, for one night only, what it felt like to be a guest at a duchess's reception in an historic house".[124]

Walter Gay, an American artist, recounted his visits to Stafford House, in letters home to his wife during the summer of 1907.[125] The most spectacular was a ball attended by Queen Alexandra:

> It was a pageant, a historical survival, and the sort of thing that only takes place in England. ... I found all the brilliant company assembled at the top of the grand staircase, awaiting the arrival of the Queen, who came soon after, with a numerous suite ... the assembled hundreds fell back to allow them to pass. As they came by the ladies curtsied and the men inclined.
> It was really very impressive ...

Gay was introduced to Strath, whom he found "an absorbed old man, who looked to be either a student or else not over bright ... I should say a timid man". Such apparent timidity did not keep him away from politics. By the 1900s Strath had become increasingly Unionist in his views: in 1906 he held a reception for the 1900 Club, a society of Unionist members of both Houses of Parliament and election candidates; and as President of the Tariff Reform League he gave at least one dinner for this movement, that in honour of Arthur Balfour.[126] As a good Unionist Sutherland was keen to foster links with colonial politicians, particularly Canadians, and held a large reception in honour of the Dominion Prime Ministers in June 1911.[127]

The Royal Family continued to attend grand receptions. King Edward VII – by now prone to ill-health – attended a ball for 500 people in June 1908 and visited the Scottish Home Industries Association Fair in July 1909. He even presented the children's governess with a hatpin, having heard that she had told them he was bound to buy one "for one of his girlfriends".[128] Perhaps the last great event in the tradition of grand Stafford House receptions was the Coronation Ball given on 19 June 1911 for the Crown princes of Europe, Turkey, Siam and Japan, at the time of the coronation of George V. Lord Stafford was paired with the Crown princess of Germany and Duchess Millicent with the Crown prince (Strath was ill at the time).

Dancing took place in the Picture Gallery and the State Dining Room. The Drawing Room and Ante-Rooms on the ground floor were used as supper rooms, and on the Terrace stood a temporary structure composed of pink, white and crimson carnations. Such a gathering would have been one of the last of its kind among European royalty before the Continent was plunged into war and before many of them or their fathers lost their thrones in the aftermath.

It was a performance several weeks later by some Apache dancers from Paris that disgusted Lord Ronald Gower and symbolized to Sir William Rothenstein the end of Sutherland supremacy. Lord Ronald Gower wrote of the last Friday soirée for artists and bohemians in his diary for 14 July 1911: "… after midnight some French dancers of the lowest café type gyrated in the Banqueting Room. People, women all round on the floor the whole thing was rather disgusting & very infradig [*sic*]."[129] Looking back after twenty years or so, Sir William Rothenstein expressed similar dismay:

> Somehow it shocked me to see the crude, sensual dances in this great house, before a ring of great ladies seated on the ground or standing in a circle round the dancers. There seemed something sinister and menacing about this invasion of *apaches* into the great Whig stronghold; I left feeling that the end of an epoch had come, that a society which admitted such dubious entertainment was somehow doomed; had indeed sentenced itself.[130]

The duchess may well have laid on such entertainment as an antidote to the stifling pomp of royalty. According to those who knew her, she looked back in later life on those gilded Edwardian days with little nostalgia.[131] On one occasion, she squirted a soda-water syphon at some lingering revellers at the end of a party.[132] Some of that spirit within her may well have induced her to put on such an avant-garde spectacle in those gilded and by now somewhat anachronistic Louis XIV surroundings.

Until the 1900s Stafford House had a sufficiently regal air and was mainly associated with such uncontroversial good causes as to place it above politics. Aspiring politicians were neither made nor broken within those gilded drawing rooms, and they were only too happy to be invited. Sovereigns from overseas could be entertained there – in a mansion so close to St James's Palace – in a way that would show off the wealth and power of Great Britain to its best advantage. Even if the last recorded gathering may have witnessed dancing of the "lowest café type", the pomp would no doubt have reasserted itself if another royal pageant had taken place before 1913. Stafford House's reputation as a palace rather than a house remained such that it was still thought the obvious place at which to entertain the kings and Crown princes who had come in June 1911 to witness the coronation of the sovereign of the largest empire in the world.

4 A "Most Celebrated Private Gallery of Art"

"The picture gallery in Stafford House", wrote Anna Jameson in 1844, "is not only the most magnificent room in London, but is also excellently adapted to its purpose, in the management of the light and decoration." Certainly, it was both the design of the Picture Gallery and its collection of Spanish paintings that ensured Stafford House's reputation as a private palace of art. "No other gallery in England", Jameson wrote, "... contains so many and various productions of this school."[1] Gustav Waagen praised them as one of the gallery's "most brilliant attractions", but he did not rate their owner as highly as the Marquis of Hertford, R.S. Holford or increasing numbers of Italian Renaissance specialists. This was mainly because the paintings at Stafford House reflected the tastes of English *cognoscenti* between the 1790s and 1830s, namely Dutch landscapes and genre paintings, and what Waagen called "the masters of the decline of Art in Italy".[2] Many of the Italian religious paintings were late Baroque, a period not favoured by mid-nineteenth-century art critics, who increasingly championed the Renaissance, particularly in its earlier stages. Indeed, the Stafford House collections could claim no monopoly of superlatives: excluding the National Gallery, the finest Dutch landscapes were to be seen in the Queen's Gallery or Sir Robert Peel's house at 4 Whitehall Gardens, and Italian paintings from Raphael onwards at Bridgewater House.[3] Both the 1st and 2nd dukes were undoubtedly active collectors. However, the 3rd duke, in order to finance the development of his vast properties in Sutherland, began the dispersal of the collection, and the 4th duke, preoccupied with the dwindling leasehold of Stafford House and Lloyd-George's fiscal policies, continued the process. After the sales of 1908 and 1913, some items made their way to Dunrobin Castle, some into public museums and galleries, but many remain untraced in private collections.

Of all four dukes, the first was probably the greatest collector: indeed he was caricatured by James Gillray as "Maecenas in pursuit of the fine Arts" (*pl. 77*),

119

hovering on the threshold of Christie's, although in fact he spent only about £1090 there. He spent almost as much at Phillips' (just over £1065),[4] and also bought from elsewhere, such as Mr Stanley's sale rooms in Maddox Street, where he purchased Murillo's *St Justa* and *St Ruffina* (*pls. 78, 81*) in June 1827 for £600, and from Michael Ryan he acquired Van Dyck's *Thomas Howard, Earl of Arundel* (Los Angeles, J. Paul Getty Museum, Rebecca Pollard Logan Collection) for just over £272. However, his most important purchases were to come from across the Channel, in the aftermath of the French Revolution. The Italian paintings of Philippe Egalité, duc d'Orléans had been purchased in Paris by M. Laborde de Merville in 1792, who brought them over to London and sold them for £40,000 to Jeremias Harman, an English banker, in order to help the royalist cause in France.[5] In June 1798 Earl Gower (as the 1st Duke of Sutherland then was), the Earl of Carlisle, his brother-in-law, and the Duke of Bridgewater, his maternal uncle, formally agreed to purchase them for £43,500.[6] From 26 December 1798 almost three hundred pictures were put up for sale: lots 1–138 were exhibited at Bryant's Gallery at 88 Pall Mall, and the remainder at the Lyceum in the Strand. Between December and April the sales reached £31,710,[7] and by February 1800 the remainder had gone for £4332. 6s. 0d.[8] Of the twenty-three pictures that Earl Gower kept for himself, nineteen would later hang in Stafford House and form the nucleus of his Italian collection. They included Paolo Veronese's *Christ and His Disciples at Emmaus* (Rotterdam, Boijmans van Beuningen Museum; *pl. 79*), Annibale Carracci's *Repose in the Flight to Egypt* (Princeton University Art Gallery) and Niccolò dell'Abbate's *Rape of Proserpine* (Paris, Musée du Louvre; *pl. 80*).

The Duke of Bridgewater died in 1803 and left his fortunes, including Cleveland House, his London residence, to his nephew, who had just become 2nd Marquis of Stafford. Between 1805 and 1806 the latter employed Charles Heathcote Tatham (1772–1842) to build a large gallery at Cleveland House, and – in an unprecedented action for an English nobleman but very much according to the precedent set by the duc d'Orléans in Paris – opened it to the public on 21 May 1806. The visiting hours were from twelve until five on Wednesdays during the London "Season" (May, June and July).[9] Here, visitors could see such masterpieces from the Orléans Gallery as Poussin's *Seven Sacraments* (Sutherland Trust, on loan to Edinburgh, The National Gallery of Scotland) and Titian's *Seven Ages of Man* and *Death of Actaeon* (London, The National Gallery). Benjamin Haydon delighted in his opportunities to study these great works, and he hailed Stafford as one of the "real supporters of the Genius of the Country".[10] Indeed, the Prince Regent toasted him at a Royal Academy dinner for his "warm desire to encourage the arts".[11] Soon after the creation of the National Gallery, Stafford donated Rubens's *Allegory of Peace*, which he had purchased from Michael Ryan in 1803 for the

Plate 77
JAMES GILLRAY (1757–1815), *Maecenas in pursuit of the Fine Arts*, 1808, etching. George Granville Leveson-Gower, 2nd Marquis of Stafford (later 1st Duke of Sutherland), was well known for his love of the arts (notwithstanding his acute short-sightedness). However, *pace* Gillray, he spent relatively modest amounts at Christie's.

Plate 78
BARTOLOMÉ ESTEBAN MURILLO
(1617–1682), *St Justa, c.* 1655, oil on
canvas, Dallas, Southern Methodist
University, Algur H. Meadows
Collection. This was bought by the 1st
Duke of Sutherland at the Altamira
sale on 1 June 1827 for £325.

Plate 79
PAULO VERONESE (1528–1588), *Christ and His Disciples at Emmaus*, c. 1570, oil on canvas, Rotterdam, Museum Boymans–van Beuningen. Formerly part of the Orléans collection.

Plate 80
NICCOLÒ DELL'ABBATE (*c.* 1509–1571),
Rape of Proserpine, c. 1560, oil on
canvas, Paris, Musée du Louvre.
Formerly part of the Orléans
collection.

Plate 81
BARTOLOMÉ ESTEBAN MURILLO
(1617–1682), *St Ruffina*, c. 1655, oil on
canvas, Dallas, Southern Methodist
University, Algur H. Meadows
Collection. This was bought by the 1st
Duke of Sutherland at the Altamira
sale on 1 June 1827 for £275.

hefty sum of £3000.[12] On the death of Lord Stafford (by then 1st Duke of Sutherland) in 1833, the Bridgewater collections passed to Lord Francis Egerton, his second son.

As early as 1827 Lord Stafford had planned to move his own paintings, 152 in number,[13] to York House and hand them down with his new residence to his eldest son.[14] There were contemporary works such as Benjamin Haydon's *Waiting for The Times* (London, The Times Collections), for which he paid £50, Francis Danby's *Passage of the Red Sea* (Preston, Harris Art Gallery) and William Etty's *Comus* (Southampton Art Gallery), for each of which he paid 500 guineas.[15] (In all three cases he paid the artist directly.) The Italian paintings that were not part of the Orléans collection included Moroni's *Titian's Schoolmaster* (Washington, DC, National Gallery of Art; *pl. 85*), bought from W. Buchanan in about 1806 for 600 guineas,[16] and Massimo Stanzione's *Italian Peasant Girl* (San Francisco, Fine Arts Museums). The Dutch school consisted of Van der Speldt's *Flowers partly hidden behind a blue curtain* (Art Institute of Chicago), and a number of landscapes and genre paintings by Van Goyen, Van Ostade and others. As there was no gallery as yet in which to display these works, they were hung in the State Apartments along the south elevation of the ground floor, the corridor and Gentleman's Room: nobody is known to have asked permission to see the pictures in their new residence.

With good reason, both Waagen and Jameson emphasized the role played by the 1st Duke of Sutherland in the history of the collecting of paintings in Great Britain. The purchase of the Orléans paintings was regarded then as being as important an acquisition for the nation as Charles I's buying of the Duke of Mantua's collection. It is very likely that Sutherland (then Earl Gower) did much to fire Bridgewater's enthusiasm. At a time when there was no National Gallery, Cleveland House provided perhaps the most important gathering-place in London for painters, *cognoscenti* and art lovers to mingle and admire the great works.

The 2nd duke very much inherited his father's love of the arts and carried on his tradition of collecting. When Gustav Waagen visited Stafford House, there was plenty for him to admire: Marshal Soult's Murillos (*pls. 88, 89*) had recently been installed in their lavish bays, specially decorated by John Henning (*pl. 83*);[17] Guercino's *St Chrysogonus Being Borne by Angels* (*pl. 2*) dominated the soffit of the lantern in the gallery, as it still does; Moroni's *Titian's Schoolmaster* was singled out "in preference to any in the whole collection".[18] Although he has proved incomparably less reticent to posterity than his father, there are, inevitably, frustrating gaps: neither Joseph Nash (*pl. 97*) nor James Digman Wingfield

Plate 82
JAMES DIGMAN WINGFIELD
(*fl.* 1832–1872), *The Picture Gallery*
[south end], *Stafford House, St James's*,
1848, oil on canvas, private collection.
The figures are not known, but the
following works of art can be
identified: *Love Among the Roses*, a
statue executed by Charles Raymond
Smith in 1835; *Madonna, Child and
Infant St John the Baptist* by Andrea del
Sarto, to the left of the doorway, with
Correggio's *The Muleteers*, formerly
part of the Orléans collection,
immediately below it; and Paul
Delaroche's *Lord Strafford on his Way
to Execution*.

Plate 83
JAMES DIGMAN WINGFIELD
(*fl.* 1832–1872), *The Picture Gallery*
[north end], *Stafford House, St James's*,
1848, oil on canvas, Paris, British
Embassy. The infant in the nurse's
arms is probably Lady Alexandrina
Leveson-Gower, who died in infancy
(Frédéric Chopin played at a reception
in honour of her christening on 15 May
1848). The large painting to the left of
the door is Niccolò dell'Abbate's *Rape
of Proserpine*, with Zurbarán's
*Madonna and Child with St John the
Baptist* immediately to the right and
Veronese's *Christ and His Disciples at
Emmaus* immediately below in the
centre. Alessandro Turchi's *Christ and
the Woman of Samaria* is to the right of
the door. As in *pl. 82*, the seating was
probably supplied by George Morant &
Son, and the chandelier by Antoine
Lynen of Paris. It is not known how the
two commodes, one (left), attr.
Philippe-Claude Montigny, now in the
J. Paul Getty Museum, Los Angeles,
and the other (right), now at Dunrobin
Castle, Sutherland, were acquired.

(*pls. 82–84*), two great recorders of Stafford House at its zenith, have left any correspondence to accompany their paintings. Precious little is known about the purchase of the above-mentioned Guercino, other than that it was brought to England from Rome by Alexander Day, presumably in about 1801,[19] and taken down from Cleveland (by now Bridgewater) House by George Morant & Son soon after December 1834.[20] Nor is it known when the *Three Graces* by Battista Zelotti was bought, although it was probably installed in the ceiling of the North-East Ante-Room (between the Picture Gallery and the Banqueting Room) between about 1836 and 1837 (*pl. 76*). Thomas Jackson, the duke's private secretary, ran a special account from February 1841, if not earlier, but only one such book (1845–55) survives.[21] Nevertheless, much is owed to Lord Ronald Gower, the youngest surviving child of the 2nd duke. He inherited his father's love of the arts and recorded selected items from the collection in a lavish folio edition, a mere three years before they were dispersed.[22]

As a young man, the 2nd duke (then known as Earl Gower) spent two years in Italy (1816–17), but his sojourn left him somewhat disappointed in terms of acquisitions: in one letter home to his mother, he "dreamt the other night my father, on seeing my little purchases, held them all rather cheap".[23] Approaches to Canova resulted in the none-too attractive offer of a marble statue of Mme Mère, Napoleon's mother, which he declined.[24] The *Venus* after Canova (Sutherland, Dunrobin Castle, Sutherland Trust), which he finally acquired in 1836, was to come from Firle, East Sussex.[25] Nevertheless, he managed to make one acquisition, which would later stand prominently in the west end of the Banqueting Room of Stafford House. In 1817 he ordered a marble *Ganymede and the Eagle* (Minneapolis Institute of Art) from Bertel Thorvaldsen, the great Danish sculptor (*pl. 86*). It was finally dispatched from Rome in July 1829, at a cost of 2000 scudi (just under £485),[26] and by about 1841 came to rest in the lavishly gilded arched recess that it would occupy until 1913.[27]

Just over a year after succeeding his father, the 2nd duke went on an eighteen-month trip to Paris (October 1835 till April 1837) and came back with his most important purchases. It was here that he bought from Marshal Soult Murillo's *Abraham Attending to the Angels* (Ottowa, National Gallery of Canada; *pl. 88*) and *The Return of the Prodigal Son* (Washington, DC, National Gallery of Art; *pl. 89*), and Paul Delaroche's history painting *Lord Strafford on his Way to Execution* (private collection; *pl. 91*. Two years earlier he had been encouraged to buy the latter's works by Lord Francis Egerton, who told him, "people fall into fits before his execution of Lady Jane Grey [London, The National Gallery] ...".[28] After seeing *Lord Strafford on his Way to Execution*, the duke hailed it as "one of the finest modern Pictures I ever saw" and proceeded to buy it for just over £183.[29] It was exhibited at the Paris Salon in 1837, and arrived at Stafford House in November 1837. Benjamin Haydon was one of the first people in England to see it, and he conveyed his well-meaning but rather tactless impressions to the duke: "In colour it wants warmth – and in flesh purity of tone – but it is a fine specimen & worthy of your Grace's patronage. The hands of men of high birth are more delicate (like Vandyke's [*sic*]) – than La Roche [*sic*] has made Strafford's."[30] However, a few days earlier, he had written despairingly in his diary: "I ask any impartial person if my Solomon, Jerusalem & Lazarus are not greater works than La Roche [*sic*] has ever done!"[31]

In March 1836 the duke made his famous purchase of Spanish paintings from Marshal Soult, the Peninsular Wars veteran. Originally presented with these works by the comte de Cuvilliers for services to his country, the marshal tried unsuccessfully to sell them to the French government but finally gave them to Sutherland for £8000,[32] allegedly half the price for which he had offered them to the Rothschilds.[33] In England, Richard Westmacott RA said it was "a great thing for this Country to Possess those pictures". The duke's mother half-jokingly warned him: "you will have no peace in your House with people coming to see

Plate 85
GIOVANNI BATTISTA MORONI (*c.* 1525 – 1578) *Titian's Schoolmaster*, oil on canvas, *c.* 1575, Washington, DC, National Gallery of Art. The 1st Duke of Sutherland (then 2nd Marquis of Stafford) purchased this work from W. Buchanan in about 1806 for 600 guineas. This was Carl Waagen's favourite work at Stafford House.

them unless you make a separate entry. – it really is a grand affair!"[34] Sutherland could now feel that he had won his spurs as a collector, and that he had made an acquisition to rival that of the Orléans Gallery. Although he refrained from comparing himself with his father, he wrote with barely disguised triumph: "tho' I cannot say 'anch' io sono Pittore', yet anch' io sono acquisitore!"[35]

In addition to paintings, the Sutherlands bought furniture and bronzes during their sojourn in Paris. Only a small portion of the former were antique: the most conspicuous example was a moderately priced secretaire that supposedly belonged to Queen Marie Antoinette. But it seems most unlikely that the famous Riesener mother-of-pearl secretaire (Chantilly, Musée Condé), once housed in the South-West Drawing Room, could have been bought for less than £6.[36] Otherwise they would seem mostly to have been modern pieces, ranging from an *étagère* made of Botany Bay wood[37] to gilt chairs and sofas in styles ranging from *à lyre* to *anciens models* or *forme Louis XV.*[38] A source of delight to the Sutherlands were the bronze foundries in the Marais: the *fondeurs* were thought "very engaging", and nowhere else in the world was there anything quite like their workshops.[39] From Antoine Lynen, who described himself as *agent commissionnaire* to the

courts of Austria and Prussia, they bought a range of bronze ornaments (*pl. 56*),[40] which included a pair of chandeliers made by Renault and a lavish ormolu clock and chimney piece by Crozatier (*pl. 104*) for the Picture Gallery. Perhaps their most glamorous item was a statue of the young Lord Stafford, modelled by J.-J. Feuchère[41] and cast by a M. Vittoz at a cost of 5500 francs (Sutherland, Dunrobin Castle, Sutherland Trust, *pl. 87*).[42] As Sutherland wrote to his mother, "Trentham [the 3rd duke's courtesy title as a small child], much to his annoyance, has been sitting for a bust, and that it is to be a statue in a Highland costume as large as himself".[43] The statue was exhibited in the Paris Salon of 1838 and proudly placed in the Green Library on arrival at Stafford House.[44]

Plate 88
BARTOLOMÉ ESTEBAN MURILLO
(1617–1682), *Abraham and the Three Angels*, 1670–74, oil on canvas, Ottawa, National Gallery of Canada. Originally from the Hospital de la Santa Caridad in Seville, and formerly part of the Marshal Soult collection.

Plate 89
Bartolomé Esteban Murillo
(1617–1682), *The Return of the Prodigal
Son*, 1667–70, oil on canvas,
Washington, DC, National Gallery of
Art. Originally from the Hospital de la
Santa Caridad in Seville, and formerly
part of the Marshal Soult collection.

Having just returned from Paris, Sutherland was persuaded by Dominic Colnaghi, the great Bond Street dealer, to buy the *cabinet Alexandre Lenoir* (died 1839). This great French antiquary had done more than anyone to save royal monuments and works of art during the upheavals of the French Revolution. The collection was composed of 69 paintings and 134 drawings, and consisted mostly of portraits of French monarchs from the Middle Ages to Louis XVI, their queens and mistresses. Having offered these works to an unwilling Musée Royal for 33,700 francs, Lenoir eventually sold them for 32,000 francs (£1266. 12s. 0d.) to Colnaghi, who in turn sold them to Sutherland for £1695. 5s. 3d., a price that included extensive restoration.[45] In an undated letter, quoted in the unpublished diaries of Lord Ronald Gower, Colnaghi wrote:

> The day after I purchased this collection in Paris I received a letter from my friend M. Sauvagent the antiquary (who left his cabinet to the French Nation). He wrote something to the effect "Vous avez acheté le Cabinet Lenoir, hélas! Voilà encore des objets du plus grand interêt historique perdu à la France et ensevelis dans ce Louvre d'Angleterre"[46]

It could be argued that these works, although included in the catalogues, were somewhat *ensevelis* (*i.e.* buried) in "apartments strictly private" at Stafford House. Although Pierre Subleyras's portrait of Pope Benedict XIV hung in the Picture Gallery, the overwhelming majority of Lenoir pictures were hung in the duke's Small Dining Room.[47] A few intrepid antiquaries, such as a Mr P. Frazer Tyler of Inverness,[48] managed to view them, as well as French historians such as Montelambert and Mérimée.[49] Lord Ronald Gower brought out a de luxe catalogue with lithographic illustrations done in his own hand, which sold precious few copies. As the critic of *The Times* said: "The Portraits not being in the picture gallery of Stafford House, but hung in some of the private rooms, are not generally seen."[50] As early as 1846 the *Art Union* correspondent wrote in slightly damning tones: "they are of much greater interest to the historian and antiquary than to the artist."

If their stay in Paris had played its part in encouraging the Sutherlands to buy the Lenoir collection, their trip to Italy from October 1838 to June 1839 inspired them – particularly the duchess – to adorn the walls of the Principal Staircase with large copies of Paolo Veronese's work (*pls. 59, 98*). The most important items they bought were bronze statues for the gardens of Trentham in the form of copies by a Signor Papi of the Pictruja *Venus* and Cellini's *Perseus*,[51] and a *Delphic Sibyl* in marble by Rinaldo Rinaldi (Buckinghamshire, Cliveden House, NT).[52] Until replaced by Marochetti's *Erin* after 1857,[53] the *Sibyl* stood on the central landing of the Principal Staircase, and is visible in the watercolours of both Eugéne Lami

Plate 90
GERARD VAN HONTHORST (1590–1658),
Christ before Caiaphas, c. 1615, oil on
canvas, London, The National Gallery.
This painting was purchased by the
2nd Duke of Sutherland from the
Society of Watercolour Painters in July
1840. Harriet Beecher Stowe wrote of
it: "It was a candlelight scene, and only
two faces were very distinct; the
downcast, calm, resolute face of Christ
... and the eager, perturbed
vehemence of the high priest who is
interrogating him ... . The presence of
this picture here in the midst of this
scene was very affecting to me."

(*pl. 72*) and Joseph Nash (*pl. 97*). While in Italy, Sutherland tried but failed to purchase from the Duke of Lucca the *Madonna della Neve* and *The Crucifix* by Guido Reni.[54] However, as if to compensate, he managed to acquire in London the duke's *Christ before Caiaphas* by Gerard van Honthorst (London, The National Gallery; *pl. 90*) in July 1840 – the painting that particularly moved Harriet Beecher Stowe when she visited Stafford House.[55]

It was probably the Sutherlands' stay in Venice that inspired Duchess Harriet to commission Giuseppe Gallo Lorenzi, a native of that city, to paint large copies of paintings by Paolo Veronese for the Principal Staircase. In addition, she may well have been told by Charles Greville (who certainly wrote as much in his diary)

Plate 91
PAUL DELAROCHE (1797–1856), *Lord Strafford on his Way to Execution*, 1834–35, oil on canvas, private collection. The painting was exhibited at the Paris Salon in 1837, having been bought the year before by the 2nd Duke, and installed in the Picture Gallery of Stafford House in November of that year.

how like a Veronese picture one of her receptions in the hall was.[56] On the south wall of the Landing (*pl. 98*) still hangs a copy of *St Sebastian Being Led to Martyrdom*, from the church of San Sebastiano in Venice. On either side are two paintings from the church of Santa Caterina in Venice: *The Mystic Marriage of St Catherine* and *The Adoration of the Shepherds*. On the opposite wall (*pl. 59*) there still hang the martyrdoms of St George, from the church of San Giorgio in Verona, and St Afra, from her church in Brescia. Between the two is an inset depicting angels, copied from a painting by Pordenone in the Accademia at Verona.

Huge sums were paid for this work. Lorenzi was able to charge 200 Napoléons d'Or (approximately £4700)[57] for the St Sebastian;[58] 240 Napoleons d'Or (approximately £5640) for the *Mystic Marriage* and *Adoration*; and, owing to expenses incurred in going beyond Venice to Verona and Brescia, 320 Napoléons (approximately £7520) for the *St George* and *St Afra* – a hefty total of nearly £18,000.[59] He finished the *St Sebastian* by December 1841. Work on the *Mystic Marriage* and *The Adoration of the Shepherds* had probably begun by June 1843[60] and was definitely completed by July 1845.[61] The *St George* had been completed and dispatched to London by April 1846 and *St Afra* by September of that year.[62] Lorenzi managed to persuade the duchess that a copy of Titian's *Assunta* placed next to *St George* would be a mistake,[63] and in the end both agreed upon Veronese's *St Afra* instead, but with corpses tastefully concealed by swirls of drapery.[64] The series was concluded with a copy of *Heads of Three Angels* (*angioletti*) by Pordenone in the Accademia at Verona: they were probably executed at the suggested price of 55 Napoléons and completed some time in 1848.[65] By June 1847 George Morant & Son had prepared at least two large frames, marbled in imitation of the surrounding scagliola.[66]

Inevitably, the Sutherlands patronized the most fashionable English portrait-painters of the day. As Earl Gower, the 2nd duke had commissioned from Sir Thomas Lawrence a full-length portrait of his wife (Sutherland, Dunrobin Castle, Sutherland Trust; *pl. 92*) towards the end of 1824. She asked for a portrait of herself seated, like that of Lady Grey. By 1827 the Gowers' eldest child, Elizabeth Georgiana, then aged three, was to be included in the portrait. This work, destined to hang in the Dining Room of Stafford House, was completed by 1828, and what started off as a 500-guinea commission ended up – following the inclusion of their daughter – as one of 650 guineas.[67] When Lawrence died a mere two years later, Earl Gower was one of the pall-bearers at his funeral.

Sir Edwin Landseer, although by no means as great a portraitist as Lawrence, was a highly successful artist who could count the Sutherlands among his

elevated clientele. His work included a large portrait of the young Marquis of Stafford and Lady Evelyn Leveson-Gower (Dunrobin Castle, Sutherland, Sutherland Trust; *pl. 94*), which was painted in 1838[68] and hung in the Green Library. The "Harmoniousness of the Colouring" of this work greatly impressed Harriet Beecher Stowe, who until then had never seen an original Landseer painting.[69] From 1844 to 1855 Landseer executed a series of insets of the duchess's four eldest children as the four seasons (*pl. 95*), which hung in her sitting room: according to Lord Ronald Gower, the portrait of Lady Caroline, later Duchess of Leinster, was not finished until she was "a mother with a large family".[70] Indeed, her portrait is not included in the 1844 catalogue.

Perhaps the most monumental portrait of Duchess Harriet was executed by Franz Winterhalter (Sutherland, Dunrobin Castle, Sutherland Trust; *pl. 93*). Although originally part of the Trentham collections, the image of the duchess proudly posing by the Principal Staircase of Stafford House most clearly evokes Queen Victoria's famous quote about coming from her house to the Sutherlands' "palace". Winterhalter's *Scene from the Decameron* (Karlsruhe, Staatliche Kunsthalle) was already hanging in the Green Library of Stafford House by 1844, but the duchess was sufficiently impressed by the artist's portrait of Queen Victoria to commission one of herself in 1849. By June, the portrait was "far advanced, though without any background": the queen, who had come specially to Stafford House to see the painting in progress, was impressed by the duchess's pose "in court dress with her train over her arm, and quite 'dans le grand style'".[71] Nevertheless, the painting probably remained unfinished until the early 1850s: it was not until 7 July 1852 that Winterhalter received his fee of 300 guineas.[72]

It was not only the duke and his family but also the interiors of his London mansion that were recorded in paint. In addition to the Winterhalter portrait, there was the Joseph Nash watercolour of the Great Hall (*pl. 97*), the Eugène Lami watercolour of a reception at Stafford House (*pl. 72*), and the three James Digman Wingfield paintings (1848) of the Picture Gallery (*pls. 82, 84, 83*).[73] Various works of art can be identified in the Wingfield paintings, such as the Delaroche painting mentioned above, Andrea del Sarto's *Madonna, Child and Infant St John the Baptist* (New York, Hunter College Museum) and Charles Raymond Smith's marble sculpture *Love Among the Roses* in the south section; Marshall Soult's Murillos in the central section; and Paolo Veronese's *Christ and His Disciples at Emmaus* and Niccolò dell'Abbate's *Rape of Proserpine* in the north section. Wingfield exhibited what could have been a single painting of the whole gallery at the British Institution (no. 292 in the catalogue) in 1849: a similar picture, *The Cartoon Gallery of Hampton Court*,[74] also by Wingfield, hung in the Ante-Dining Room on the ground floor of Stafford House. Joseph Nash's watercolour of the hall, although undated and undocumented, was probably done either then or during the early 1850s, about the time when he painted the Waterloo Gallery of Apsley House (1852; *pl. 48*). In the case of Eugène Lami, it was largely owing to a minor contretemps with royalty that he has been recorded. On the day that the queen came to see the Winterhalter portrait, she met the French artist at work on his watercolour of the staircase. Not knowing who she was, Lami proceeded firmly to disagree with her on the subject of Lamartine's *History of the Girondins*. The duchess had to retrieve the situation by quietly pointing out to whom he was talking.[75] The queen overlooked the incident: without any hint of disparagement, she referred to him in her journal as "the clever French artist".[76]

The 2nd Duke of Sutherland inherited his father's reputation for buying works of art and supporting artists in the metropolis. Between 1835 and his death in 1861 he served as a (none-too-active) trustee of the National Gallery.[77] His charities included the Artists' Benevolent Fund for the Relief of their Widows and Orphans, and he received his share of harrowing letters from artists reduced to dire poverty.[78] When "declining health and lack of commissions" compelled John Francis, the sculptor, to offer various busts for sale, the duke agreed to purchase *Lord John Russell*, *Queen Victoria* and *The Prince Consort*.[79] Perhaps the most burdensome artist of all was Benjamin Haydon. The 2nd duke paid him 25 guineas for the *Cartoon of Edward the Black Prince* in 1844[80] and 400 guineas for a large painting of *Cassandra Foretelling the Death of Hector* in about 1835.[81] Nevertheless, Haydon forever hovered on the threshold of poverty and the debtor's prison. The duke bore with his eccentricities and summed up his feelings on an envelope containing his letters: "Letters from poor Mr Haydon at various times ... he was not ungrateful for favours, I now wish that I had done more for him but I doubt if more would have availed altogether."[82]

As well as commissioning works of art, the 2nd duke bought directly from artists and mostly dealers, but comparatively little from auctioneers. Other than buying Pannini's *Marriage at Cana* (Louisville, Kentucky, J.P. Speed Museum) and four Dutch paintings (three landscapes by Van Goyen, Moucheron, Pynacker and a *Skirmish of Cavalry* by Van der Meulen)[83] from the duc de Berry's sale (25 April 1834), his purchases from Christie's did not exceed £50.[84] Serendipity also played its part: in the case of John Lough's (untraced) marble statue of *Ariel*, the duke happened to stumble upon a work or art that at the price of £650 proved an ideal "birthday Marriage day & ca present" for the duchess, and one worthy of the Picture Gallery.[85] One of his more important suppliers was George Morant & Son, who in 1847 sold the duke *The Holy Family* by Fra Bartolomeo for 80 guineas,[86] and in 1846 gave the duchess Albani's *The Triumph of Ariadne* in exchange for ten of her pictures.[87] This action gave rise to rumours in Society – much to James Loch's dismay – that the Sutherlands could not pay Morant's bills and were in serious financial difficulties.[88]

Stafford House was cluttered with an abundance of *objets d'art*. Bronze statuettes were purchased from Susse Frères in Paris (as well as from Antoine Lynen) and from M. Crozatier, who had originally supplied pieces to Lynen and had set up business in London by 1848.[89] There were also large amounts of china, both domestic and decorative, bought from Minton & Co. Duchess Harriet greatly admired their work and became a close friend of Herbert Minton: she went with him and her brother to the Exposition Universelle in Paris in 1855.[90] They presented the Princess Royal with a set of Minton Ware Majolica vases on her marriage to Crown Prince Friedrich Wilhelm.[91] The Sutherlands' most lavish purchase of silverware was perhaps a Hydra candelabra, supplied by Emmanuel & Son[92] and prominently displayed in the State Dining Room when the Emperor of Prussia visited Stafford House in February 1842.[93]

Although the 1st duke (or Earl Gower, as he then was) served as ambassador to France between August 1790 and November 1792, he bought disappointingly little while he was there:[94] unlike William Beckford, he did not have the time. (There was another visit to Paris in 1821,[95] but bills from this period have been lost.) As far as we know, antique French furniture was mostly bought not from Paris but from London dealers-cum-cabinetmakers such as E.H. Baldock: pieces from the latter included a "very rich gilt table made to fit circular plaque of china"[96] and an ormolu clock by Le Paute, which Alfred de Rothschild was to buy in 1876 (see below).[97] George Morant & Son supplied "two richly carved & gilt chairs (formerly Marie Antoinette's)" for £18. 14s. 0d.: these had come from Desiré Dellier's bankruptcy sale. In addition, the 2nd duke inherited various pieces of Boulle furniture, including a monumental writing desk, from Thomas Grenville.[98] Although precious few bills can be traced, the 1839 inventory indicates an abundance of rich furniture that could well have been French or at least a confection à la Baldock in that style: five dwarf *pietre dure* commodes "of marble & ormolu ornamented with polished stones with columns of fine jasper and the tops of rose jasper" (p. 45 of inventory); a mother-of-pearl *escritoire*; a library table set with Sèvres plaques (p. 52 of inventory); and a series of Buhl cabinets with marble tops in the gallery (p. 58 of inventory). In addition, there was an abundance of French ormolu clocks in the various drawing rooms and libraries.

Both of the first two dukes were avid collectors of books. The 1st duke had a large number on the fine arts, including a first edition of Vasari's *Vite degli Artisti* (1568), as well as catalogues of the various Royal Collections and, among others, those of Mr Angerstein, later to form the nucleus of the National Gallery. No

Plate 94
SIR EDWIN LANDSEER (1802–1873),
*The Marquis of Stafford and Lady
Evelyn Leveson-Gower*, 1838, oil on
canvas, Sutherland, Dunrobin Castle,
Sutherland Trust. This painting hung
in the Green Library, Lancaster House,
where "the Harmoniousness of the
Colouring" particularly impressed
Harriet Beecher Stowe.

doubt he referred to the *Diccionario de las Bellas Artes en España* when contemplating buying the Murillos from the Altamira sale.[99] The 2nd Duke of Sutherland shared his father's wide range of interests: his purchases ranged from Perelle's *Les Délices de Versailles* to incunabula such as Tasso's *Gerusalemme liberata* (Venice 1609) and Cicero's *Tusculae quaestiones* (Paris 1558).[100] He also possessed a copy of A. Lenoir's *Musée imperial des monuments français* (Paris 1810), which he must have pored over before purchasing the Lenoir collection.[101] The 2nd duke's purchase of prints included *La Galerie de Versailles*,[102] Rauch's *Sculptures* and Schinkel's *Möbel Entwurfe*.[103] No doubt the latter publication inspired him to order for his Picture Gallery a copy of a sofa, decorated with reclining putti, that Schinkel had made for the Crown princess of Prussia.[104]

The 2nd duke shared his father's tastes for Italian, Flemish and Spanish works, and he bought from the Soult, de Berry and Lucca collections, much as the 1st duke would have done had he still been alive. The duchess, in choosing to decorate the Principal Staircase with Veronese copies, helped create the air of sixteenth-century Venetian opulence that so impressed Queen Victoria and Charles Greville. While displaying a penchant for the grand effect, the duchess's tastes were often somewhat squeamish and mawkish. Both Lorenzi and John Martin expunged corpses from their religious paintings. Martin agreed to exclude "those details which would be revolting to the eye and good taste" from his *Assuaging the Flood* (San Francisco, Museum of Fine Art): pretty seashells were thought more decorous.[105] Queen Victoria took the somewhat bizarre idea of collecting sculpted marble limbs of her small children (Isle of Wight, Osborne House, English Heritage) from seeing the hand of Lady Constance Leveson-Gower sculpted by Abraham Kent.[106] Nevertheless, Duchess Harriet remained enamoured of building: this factor, combined with dwindling income from the railways, necessitated fewer purchases of art for Stafford House. As if to gain the approval of James Loch, the duke wrote in 1852: "I have avoided any pictures or anything in London that would lead me to expense."[107] Although such well-intentioned acts of self-denial did not produce the savings desired, at least the 2nd duke's death did not force upon his heir any massive sales or curtailment in lavish living.

The creation of the Stafford House Picture Gallery, the purchase of the Murillos, and reports on royal visits in the court pages of the press helped spread the reputation of the 2nd Duke of Sutherland's collection. The report in *The Times* on the visit of the King of Prussia in February 1842 referred to "the New Gallery ... which is too well known to require even an attempt at description in our limited space."[108] When Anna Jameson brought out her *Companion* in 1844, she stated that it was a "*private* collection, to which admission is obtained only by

express invitation". In the early stages, someone as prominent as Lord Brougham was remarkably diffident when enquiring on behalf of a friend: "Don't be alarmed!", he began his letter.[109] Once Anna Jameson's book had been published, the number of requests seem to have increased. By April 1845 the Duke of Sutherland had written a memorandum that allowed admission only to his acquaintances "during the full season", while he was in residence.[110] However, by 1848 the duchess took a more liberal view, and stated that "any one wishing to see our house should see it".[111] Indeed, by June 1851, the duke's private secretary was writing to James Loch: "The rule is so far relaxed that persons who have any introduction or are well known are admitted on Saturday afternoons between 5 and 7, but the duke does not exactly publish that for fear of too many applications."[112] During the winter, the walls and furniture of the gallery – like the State Apartments – were covered up, and visits discouraged.

Those who applied ranged from members of the public to foreign dignitaries. In June 1887 the Queen of Hawaii, "a swarthy, jolly, intelligent dame",[113] was given a tour of the Gallery by Lord Ronald Gower, as was a party of Americans the next month – "all most delighted with the house".[114] However, not all were impressed: the young Henry Cole thought the gilded interiors "more gorgeous than tasteful";[115] Ford Madox Brown was disgusted by "such heaping up of bad taste [and] such gilding of hideousness".[116] Some visitors could be troublesome: a Mr Sayer, having initially been refused permission to copy the Murillos, managed to worm his way in through acquaintances of George Loch and ensconce himself there for three months: Duchess Annie, we are told, "was much bored & annoyed by the obstruction he made in the house".[117] By the 1900s it was mostly Americans who applied for admission to Stafford House.[118] By then, the house had become something of a tourist attraction, helped by such events as the Stafford House Lifeboat Fête in June 1901, and the annual sales of the Scottish Home Industries Association in the garden. In July 1910 the Duke of Sutherland admitted 603 members of the National Sunday League. What began as admission for the few *cognoscenti* and the acquaintances of the Sutherlands became increasingly democratic.

The pictures were hung much as they would have been a century earlier. As Wingfield's paintings show, they were arranged symmetrically and fairly densely packed from the dado to the uppermost picture rail, and stayed put until about 1907. Gustav Waagen complained that individual pictures, such as two portraits by Titian and the *Madonna, Child and Infant St John the Baptist* by Andrea del Sarto, were displayed in such a way that he could not judge their authenticity. It is not known who (if anyone) other than the 2nd duke and Duchess Harriet arranged the hang – no evidence has come to light to indicate that Barry had a hand in it. As far as we can judge, the paintings moved little from the time of the creation of the Picture Gallery in 1841 until the "weeding out' of pictures in 1907 (see below). Unlike the 1st duke's picture hang at Bridgewater House, the pictures were divided by school only to a limited extent: the Ante-Room to the west of the Lower Drawing Room was hung mostly with Dutch and Flemish paintings and the one to the east exclusively with English works. The dominant school in the Picture Gallery was Italian, but exceptions to the rule included Van Dyck's *Earl of Arundel* and *Lucas Van Uffelen*, Delaroche's *Lord Strafford*, and (after 1907) the Trentham Romneys. Otherwise, different schools and styles were mixed with far more freedom than they had been at Bridgwater House. Pordenone's *Woman Taken in Adultery* was hung in the Lower Dining Room with Sir Thomas Lawrence's *Countess Gower and her Daughter*; Guido Reni's *Atalanta and Hippomenes* with Sir Edwin Landseer's *Lord Stafford and Lady Evelyn Leveson-Gower* in the Green Library. The 2nd duke did not rigorously follow his father's method of hanging pictures by school; but then, they formed what was essentially a private collection and not a semi-public gallery, where more heed would have been paid to the latest fashions in picture hanging.

With the passing of the 2nd duke, Stafford House neither acquired any important works on the level of the Orléans collection or the Soult collection, nor did it foster any artistic movement like, for example, the Pre-Raphaelites. 'Staff', the 3rd duke, was a man of boundless energy, but not as great a collector or patron of artists as his father. He lent his time and influence to a number of causes to do with the arts, and provided Stafford House as a magnificent setting for the committee meetings that went with them. He held a lavish banquet for Her Majesty's Commissioners for the International Exhibition of 1862;[119] and he chaired at least one meeting for the debenture holders of the New Opera House.[120] His interest in archaeology led him to purchase and open up a mummy

Plate 96
View of the State Drawing Room (also known as the Great South Drawing Room), photographed by Bedford Lemère, Stafford House, 1895, with the statue of Eve by Odoardo Fantacchiatti visible in front of the window, and a large gilt dolphin table, supplied by E.H. Baldock in 1837.

at Stafford House, in the presence of Sir Henry Cole, S. Birch of the British Museum and Professor Owen, a distinguished surgeon.[121] Birch borrowed some of his stone rubbings in order to investigate a series of 'Moabite' fakes.[122] Staff also probably bought several cassoni (Indianapolis Museum of Art) from the great Anglo-Florentine dealer William Blundell Spence.[123]

Nevertheless, his commissioning or collecting of work would seem to have been largely confined to sculpture: commemorative busts, statues and effigies of his parents by Matthew Noble,[124] a marble group entitled *The Crescent Moon* by C.G. Cali (*pl. 69*)[125] and a marble statue of *Eve* by Odoardo Fantacchiatti (*pl. 96*).[126] Sir Henry Cole twice recounted in his diaries meeting Mlle Debay (*sic*), "a French sculptress", who was then making a bust of his daughter Lady Alexandra.[127] In addition to an anonymous bust of the latter in the Grand Hall, the 1896 inventory lists *Jeptha's Daughter*, portrait busts of the 3rd duke, the Prince Impérial and a self-portrait by Charlotte Dubray (assuming she was the same person as Mlle Debay).[128] Besides sculpture, there was one painted portrait of Duchess Annie by Sir Frederick Grant at Stafford House and another by A. Bassano (1877) at Dunrobin (*pl. 101*), and an R. Herdman portrait of the duke, proudly displaying the plans for his costly agricultural schemes at Lairg (1877) that helped bring about the beginning of the dispersal of the collections.

Even if the 3rd duke was not an active collector, his pictures were freshly catalogued and cleaned when necessary; he was prepared to lend to exhibitions; and as early as 1882 he experimented with newfangled electricity to light up the gallery, which until then had been illuminated by gas burners placed outside

the glass panes of the lantern. Cumbersome and unreliable as this source of
power was in the 1880s, Staff, with his love for technological innovations, was
among the first to illuminate a gallery, public or private, with electricity. In 1868
an anonymous but more comprehensive catalogue than that of 1844 was
published: it listed some 248 paintings in the upper and lower State Apartments
and corridors on the ground floor. Henry Wright, the duke's private secretary,
employed Richard Smart to clean and revarnish pictures, and on occasions
research their history. In 1879 Smart worked on the Lorenzi paintings in the
Principal Staircase, which had been "damaged by the sun".[129]

Given the reputation of the Stafford House collections, it was inevitable that
they were often in demand for exhibitions. When the indefatigable Sir Henry Cole
mounted the Art Exhibition and Bazaar at Alton Towers in aid of the Wedgwood
Memorial Institute in 1865, George Loch somewhat tartly remarked: "At the
present moment the duke would hardly like to denude Stafford House of any of
the Pictures".[130] At the request of the ever-persuasive Joe Comyns Carr, owner of
the New Gallery and friend of Sir Edward Burne-Jones, he lent Winterhalter's
Harriet, Duchess of Sutherland to the Victoria exhibition in 1891.[131] Carr habitually
requested considerably more paintings than the duke was prepared to lend.

Nevertheless, the 3rd duke began the process of selling off the collection.
In order to develop his vast estates, Staff invested huge sums of money in farm

reclamation at Lairg and in a colliery, brick shops and saw mills at Brora. To finance these costly schemes, he borrowed from Drummonds and the Aberdeen Town and Country Banks, and sold investments. In addition, in 1876 he sold the Lenoir collection (to the duc d'Aumale) for £8000 and "other articles from Stafford House" for £14,500.[132] Lord Ronald Gower tried to persuade his elder brother to present the Lenoir collection to the Louvre, but to no avail.[133] Less than seven years later it was acquired by the Musée Condé, Chantilly. Alfred de Rothschild purchased the "other articles" through E. Joseph, a Bond Street dealer.[134] These included two paintings by Watteau, the Le Paute clock from E.H. Baldock and Marie Antoinette's mother-of-pearl secretaire, made by Jean-Henri Riesener (Chantilly, Musée Condé).[135] Thus began the dispersal, albeit on quite a small scale, of the Sutherland collections. No other sales are recorded within the 3rd duke's lifetime. In spite of the upheavals that followed his father's second marriage (see next chapter), the 4th duke was able to hold on well into the 1900s. It was to be the sale of the properties from 1907 until 1913 – and the contents that went with them – that caused the break up of the Stafford House collections. 'Strath', the 4th Duke of Sutherland, showed comparatively little enthusiasm for commissioning or collecting works of art. Granted, in 1898 he sat in the State Dining Room for a portrait by Hubert von Herkomer (*pl. 75*), which was presented by the "Members of his Estates, Farmers and Supporters". Nor could he be accused of complete philistinism: like his father, he took care of his pictures, and entrusted those in need of restoration to Stephen Richards; John Singer Sargent was commissioned to execute a full-length portrait (Madrid, Museo Thyssen-Bornemisza) and a charcoal sketch of Duchess Millicent (*pl. 74*), exhibited at the Royal Academy in 1904 and 1905 respectively.[136] Furthermore, when making introductory conversation with his future wife at Dunrobin, he was struck by the fact that a girl of fourteen could recognize a Romney at sight, and thereafter lost all interest in her older sister.[137] As his wife, Duchess Millicent was remembered by her contemporaries as a glamorous hostess, famous for her parties where painters congregated with politicians. For posterity she is flatteringly recorded in art by John Singer Sargent and in prose by Sir William Rothenstein. However, her energies were more taken up with supporting such concerns as the Silk Association and the Scottish Home Industries Associations than commissioning new works of art.

Nevertheless, Liberal governments before the First World War were less sympathetic to the landed interest than the Tory and Whig governments of the 1820s and 1830s. Driven on by apprehension of the future and a defeatism that exasperated Duchess Millicent (see next chapter), the 4th duke sold off his properties and most of the contents with them. Having disposed of the contents of Trentham by November 1906, Strath undertook a "weeding" of paintings from Stafford House and Lilleshall as well (Christie's, 8 February 1908), and raised a total of £7644. 4s. 6d.[138] Haydon's *Cartoon of Edward the Black Prince* was sold for a paltry 3 guineas; his *Cassandra Foretelling the Death of Hector* for a mere 5 guineas. Danby's *The Assuaging of the Waters* sold for only 14 guineas, but Etty's *Comus* fetched £261.[139] The result of this "weeding" was the introduction of the Romneys from Trentham to the Picture Gallery, thus giving the collection – at any rate in the eyes of Gabriel Mourey[140] – a much more "English" flavour.

The main sale of pictures took place at Christie's on Friday 11 July 1913 and raised a total of £18,099.[141] The Orléans, Lucca and Altamira collections went, and much of the Soult collection, leaving the Sutherlands with the cream of the family portraits, now mostly at Dunrobin Castle, and Soult's Murillos. The latter were to be sold by the 5th duke of Sutherland to Agnew's in 1948. Of the Orléans pictures, Paolo Veronese's *Christ and His Disciples at Emmaus* was sold to Agnew's for £1417. 10s. 0d.; of the Lucca collection, Van Honthorst's *Christ before Caiaphas* fetched a mere £65; but Murillo's *St Justina* and *St Ruffina* reached 2200 guineas. Paul Delaroche's *Lord Strafford on his Way to Execution* was sold for 300 guineas. The furniture and sculpture were sold by Knight, Frank & Rutley during a three-day sale that took place on 14, 15 and 25 July 1913. C.R. Smith's *Love Among the Roses* (*pl. 82*), which had been executed in 1835 for £294,[142] fetched a mere 11 guineas.[143] Thorvaldsen's *Ganymede* (lot 384) was sold for 230 guineas and Marochetti's *Erin* (lot 369) for 105. Sir William Lever bought for the nation a series of candelabra from various state rooms and a large amount of dining-room furniture; but he kept for himself the Romilly globe clock (lot 83, 125 guineas: Merseyside, Lady Lever Art Gallery). Thanks to a Treasury grant, a substantial amount of luxurious gilt seating, original to the house, was kept *in situ* – no doubt with government hospitality very much in mind.[144] During 29–31 October 1913 the Stafford House Library was sold for a total of £2648. 2s. 6d.[145] The most expensive item was Colonel Gordon's *Collection of 387 very clever coloured drawings of quadrupeds, plants ... indigenous to South Africa* (lot 445), and this went for £690. Memories of the Boer War must have played their part in boosting the bids. However, those of the Lenoir collection had become so dim that his *Musée impérial des monuments français* (lot 326) went for only nine shillings. Thus ended a series of sales that stripped Stafford House of almost all of its collections and much of its original fittings and furniture. The 4th duke's death on 27 June 1913 spared him the doleful spectacle of such a dispersal. At least, as one who so loved Canada, he might have been consoled to hear that Murillo's *Abraham Attending to the Angels* was to find a home in the National Gallery of Canada, Ottawa, in 1949.

Of the Stafford House paintings, only those battened to the ceilings and the walls of the Principal Staircase remain, pale reminders of what had been there until 1913. However, by 1900 visitors were seeing only the glories of past collecting, the flavour of which had been established by the 1st and 2nd dukes. Once those pictures, so sought after in about 1800 but rather neglected by 1900, had been removed from their magnificent setting to the sale rooms, they lost much of their glamour – hence the *Times* correspondent's understandable but mistaken belief that only lesser works were being sold. Until July 1913 Stafford House held one of the most important private galleries of paintings assembled when richer Britons had the cream of European Old Masters at their disposal. By 1913 this enviable position was enjoyed by Americans, and it is mostly in the public collections of that country that Stafford House paintings have surfaced.

5 From Stafford House to Lancaster House

The coming of the twentieth century, particularly the aftermath of the First World War, heralded the end of the great London town house. Indeed, the first important house to be sold was Stafford House, and this was a good twelve months before the onset of the carnage that wiped out so many sons and heirs and wrought such havoc upon the old, established families. However, even before August 1914 there were those who, like Strath, thought that the great days had passed for ever and that the future, war or no war, was far from rosy. As early as July 1911, he was seriously considering selling the lease of Stafford House back to the Crown,[1] and nine months later Duchess Millicent was writing in despairing tones to Lord Esher:

> Strath has a mad lust for destruction on the plea of death duties. Never is there another phrase in his mouth ... I shall have to leave Stafford House ... I can't live without lovely things around me, associated historically with the past. Strath lives in rooms with nouveau art [*sic*] furniture bought on the hire system, I feel as if my heart were breaking at this last blow ... S. is a pitiable figure, mooning about like Scrooge and muttering about money.[2]

How had it come about that the Sutherlands, renowned for their vast resources, were reduced to selling the lease of their "palace" twenty-eight years before it expired? First of all, despite intensive lobbying early in 1841, the 2nd Duke of Sutherland had failed to secure the freehold of Stafford House: Lord Melbourne, the Prime Minister of the day, adamantly refused to persuade Queen Victoria to part with any piece of Crown property on a permanent basis.[3] Therefore, in unfavourable circumstances, a lease with only twenty-eight years to run by 1912 could easily have proved a liability. And unfavourable the circumstances were: the Liberal governments leading up to the First World War were considered unsympathetic; the Sutherland resources had been diminished by generations of heavy spending, aggravated by destructive family quarrels; and Strath ended up with no inclination to keep Stafford House.

Plate 99
Chimney piece depicting Autumn and Winter in the former South-West Drawing Room (also known as the Green Velvet Room), Lancaster House, by RICHARD WESTMACOTT THE YOUNGER RA (1799–1872). Westmacott had finished and been paid £266. 18s. 0d. for this work by June 1837.

Easy as it might be with hindsight to regard the Edwardian era as the Indian summer of the British aristocracy, it certainly did not seem so in 1909, the year of the 'People's Budget'. David Lloyd-George, the radical Chancellor of the day, set about raising taxation in order to pay for old-age pensions and the eight dreadnoughts needed to counter the threat of the expanding Imperial German Navy. Legacy and succession duties went up from 3% to 5%; a 15% surcharge was to be raised on estate duty over £15,000, and an extra 6*d*. (2½p) on incomes over £5000 to be paid on every pound over the first £3000. Although mild in comparison with the budgets that immediately followed the Second World War, it was seen as an attack on the landed interests. Indeed, the 1909 budget provoked a series of battles between the Lords and the Commons, to be settled only by the Parliament Act of 1911, which put an end to the Lords' rights to veto financial measures. In the charged atmosphere of the time, Lord Rosebery denounced the People's Budget as "a Revolution, a social and political revolution of the first magnitude";[4] and Sutherland concentrated on attacking "The Ungotten Tax" in a letter to *The Standard* (5 July 1909): this budget, in his view, would make it possible neither for landowners to make the necessary investments needed to extract those "ungotten minerals" from their estates nor for him to continue paying his staff's wages and pensions at the same level as in the past. The fiery rhetoric of Lloyd-George against the landed interest, the stormy general election of 1910, and the emasculating effect of the Parliament Act on the House of Lords left the duke – and, indeed, so many other peers – thoroughly demoralized. By 1912 he would seem to have abandoned hope and obsessed himself with death duties, Lloyd-George's most lethal fiscal weapon, to an extent that Duchess Millicent found incomprehensible.

Nevertheless, the Sutherlands could not lay all their financial woes at Lloyd-George's feet. The 2nd duke and duchess's love of building had preoccupied James Loch as early as the 1830s. The 3rd duke may have been spared his parents' urge to build, but his enthusiasm for the latest technology, coupled with what the press saw as an urge to make amends for the Highland Clearances, led him to sink huge sums into developing the county of Sutherland. The most expensive project, and one into which he would sink £250,000, was land reclamation in Lairg, Sutherland. Steam pumps were used to drain the poor, marshy soil: the 3rd duke's excessive enthusiasm for steam engines – he even drove his own trains – may well have blinded him to the commercial unviability of such a scheme. Indeed, most of his business activities, ranging from coal mines in Staffordshire to railways throughout Sutherland and brick kilns in Brora, tell a tale of over-investment, with few returns.

An article in the radical paper *Truth* (24 May 1888) announced that Stafford House would soon be up for sale. Staff's income had been reduced owing to the

"Agricultural Depression" and an "unfortunate speculation", presumably his schemes at Lairg, and he was finding it "inconvenient to maintain so huge and costly a residence". Although Staff was spending less time at Stafford House by the mid-1880s, there is no evidence that he planned to sell it. Fortunately, the article made no reference to the fact that he was spending less time with Duchess Annie (who was destined to die in six months' time) and more with Mary Caroline Blair, the wife of an Indian Civil Servant (*pl. 100*). How much healthier Strath's finances would have been without the machinations of Mrs Blair remains unknown. In the event, the heir to the Sutherland fortunes would have to contend with a reduced fortune and the animosity of his father's mistress, turned wicked stepmother.

Staff's relationship with his wife bore the marks of marrying in haste and repenting at leisure. On 27 June 1849, aged only twenty, he married Annie Hay Mackenzie, whose father owned large estates in the county of Cromartie. The fact that she was an heiress may well have helped forestall any misgivings on the part of his parents, not that they seem to have had that many. Indeed, during the lifetime of the 2nd duke, the marriage seems to have been happy: he was very fond of his daughter-in-law, and wrote her plenty of affectionate letters, on matters ranging from his frustration at his deafness to the death of Earl Gower, her eldest son, in 1857. However, like his friend the Prince of Wales, Staff had a roving eye, and he turned to courtesans such as Mme Giulia Barucci.[5] Whatever he may have lavished on paramours, by about 1867 he was becoming exasperated by his wife's tendency to overspend and would not consider increasing her allowance: "I think £1,000 a year is enough for any woman, I have no idea of increasing it", he informed George Loch.[6] As her wistful letters to George Loch show, the unfortunate Duchess Annie seriously considered securing extra loans to pay off pressing debts rather than talking matters over with her husband.[7] All too aware that the duke's attentions were wandering elsewhere during the 1880s, she gradually became more eccentric and reclusive at Stafford House: she would languish under an eiderdown on a chaise longue, surrounded by animals, dining almost exclusively off chicken and pinning fake medals on her servants.[8] In addition, she spent much time at Sutherland Heights in Torquay, a "horribly dull house" in the eyes of her husband;[9] and she consoled herself with religious instruction from the Revd Hewett, who would be at her deathbed with her brother-in-law, Lord Ronald Gower. The latter wrote of her:

> In Annie I have lost a most true, dear and never ending friend ... her life
> was not at all a bright one, always. Possibly to the outer world hers might
> have been considered such; but she had many troubles & worries;
> aggravated poor dear by a great want of tact! – She had bright qualities,
> a sweet generous heart and an ever open hand.[10]

From Gower's funerary pen-portrait, a picture is formed of a most well-meaning woman (*pl. 101*), but one whose lack of tact – not to mention fading looks – doubtless helped aggravate her husband's infidelities.

In October 1882 a Mr and Mrs Blair were entertained for a fortnight in the duchess's absence at Dunrobin.[11] Six months later, the recently widowed Mary Caroline Blair was staying with the duke at Stafford House. The daughter of the Revd Richard Michell, Public Orator and Professor of Logic at Oxford, she had married her cousin Captain Arthur Kindersley Blair in 1872, and from about 1883 she became more intimate with the duke. She and her daughter Irene went on yachting trips with him: these included voyages to the Mediterranean, Florida, Siam and the West Indies (whence they took home with them the unfortunate Charlie Stair of St Kitts).[12] While they were both staying in New York, Duchess Annie died in her bed at Stafford House on 26 November 1888. The duke's children were bitterly disappointed that, despite their pleading telegrams, he used the stormy Atlantic weather and the fact that he could "be of no use or comfort" as an excuse not to return to be with his wife in her last hours.[13] Their disappointment gave way to horror when three weeks after their mother's death he announced his intention to marry Mrs Blair. In spite of Strath's pleas that he should return to England and not marry "for some time", the wedding took place in Dunedin, Florida, on 4 March 1889, with the Bishop of Florida officiating.[14]

On the return of the newly married couple, little attempt was made by the duke's children to accommodate their stepmother. Duchess Mary Caroline would later claim that Lady Alexandra Leveson-Gower had removed all her mother's property from Stafford House, and her stepson countered by claiming that the new duchess had filched almost all of their mother's belongings from her house in Torquay.[15] She even purloined Duchess Annie's clothes, which had been intended for Lady Alexandra, and, much to the disgust of her stepchildren, took to wearing her old underwear. Duchess Mary Caroline tried to bully her stepdaughter into living under the same roof as her in order to bestow social respectability upon her.[16] Lady Alexandra did what she could to avoid doing so: she even enrolled as a probationary nurse at St Bartholomew's Hospital from May 1890.[17] The loyal daughter retained her love for her father, but, worn down by quarrels with her stepmother and dispirited by her father's compliance with his new wife, she became ill in February 1891 and died two months later.

However, the son and daughter-in-law lived to keep up the quarrel, which largely centred on Duchess Annie's last words. In a fit of pique, Strath admitted that his mother knew that her husband and his mistress would marry, and that she "hoped all would be peaceful and happy after", which Duchess Mary Caroline interpreted as including her as well. He subsequently denied that any such

Plate 100
'The late Mary Caroline, Duchess of Sutherland [died 1912]', from *Illustrated London News*, 1912. Having been the 3rd Duke of Sutherland's mistress since about 1883, she married him in 1889, four months after the death of Duchess Annie. She was detested by her stepchildren and referred to by Lord Ronald Gower as "Duchess Blair" or the "she-devil".

conversation had taken place:[18] his uncle, Lord Ronald, who had been at her deathbed, wrote " ... she trusted that if she had done any wrong it was unwittingly & that she hoped she would be forgiven as she forgave him [her husband] any offence due to her".[19] The 'forgive-us-our-trespasses' sentiment had been cleverly twisted, and was to become a great cause of animosity between stepson and stepmother, the latter of whom was busy manipulating her husband into doing his heir out his inheritance. Could the situation have been averted by more diplomacy on Strath's part? Quite possibly, but by the standards of the time his behaviour was reasonable: it was deeply hurtful to his children that Staff should have dallied in New York with Mrs Blair (as she then was) while their mother was dying, and then, without any semblance of mourning, proceeded to marry her in Florida four months later.

What his stepmother called "a war to the knife between us"[20] continued unabated: Strath and his wife boycotted the annual parties given for the tenantry by the duke and duchess at Lilleshall; he also took his father to court over the felling – at the duchess's instigation – of excessive numbers of ornamental trees at Trentham; the duke retaliated by cutting off his allowance of £1000 for the upkeep of Lilleshall and thus driving him out. A dispute over Duchess Mary Caroline's being given a house at Cambusmore, Sutherland, resulted in Strath attempting to be bought out of the entailed Scottish estates, as he saw this action as heralding their gradual break up.[21] However, by July 1892 the warring parties were nearing a compromise: Strath was prepared to concede Cambusmore to the duchess and take Lilleshall in return.[22] Seven weeks later his solicitor, Richard Taylor, wrote: "The duke was anxious as far as possible to renew friendly relations with you, and ... [was] chafing under his present influence tho' he had not sufficient strength to resist it."[23]

For all the talk of reconciliation, the will that was drawn up on 22 September 1892, six days before the duke's death, reopened wounds. To Strath (now the 4th duke) it seemed that his stepmother had been left with "almost a million and a half". He confided to his uncle, Lord Ronald Gower, that had his father lived another year he would have been ruined. In the current circumstances, Stafford House would have to be either let or sold.[24] Indeed, he even entertained the idea of letting both the London house and Dunrobin to Lord Iveagh, the Guinness brewing magnate, for a year.[25] The reversal of Sutherland fortunes was widely felt in court circles. Queen Victoria wrote to Strath:

> ... It is too dreadful to think of former times and of the very high position your Grand Parents held and of the terrible change this bad and wicked woman wrought with your father, formerly so kind and so generous, and so warm hearted.[26]

However, he was encouraged by both his solicitor and his private secretary, who under the previous will had stood to gain a pension of £600 a year, to go to court. The will certainly had two particularly menacing clauses: Strath would be cut out unless he paid his father's legacies to his grandchildren and his servants out of his own pocket; and unless he toed the line with his stepmother, she was free not to bequeath him his father's personal estate. Nevertheless, the clauses were held to have no legal effect.[27] Duchess Mary Caroline published a pamphlet that attacked her stepchildren, only to become "terribly frightened" that she might be sued for libel.[28] However, the new duke retaliated by contesting the will on the grounds that she had used undue influence and fraud to set her husband against his own children in order that she could acquire all his personal property. Whether he would have won his case is a matter for speculation. The dowager duchess certainly made a serious blunder in burning one of her husband's letters at the office of the administrator of this case in March 1893.[29] This rash action landed her in Holloway Prison from 18 April until 29 May 1893. The idea of a duchess ending up in prison naturally excited the interest of the press, and questions about her treatment were asked in Parliament.[30] Classified as a misdemeanant (rather than a criminal), she was allowed her own food, furniture, clothing and even one servant.[31] She was treated by the prison doctor for an enlarged heart, and on 29 May 1893 she was released on health grounds. She may have been called "the she-devil" and "Duchess Blair" by Lord Ronald Gower and his cousins, but she succeeded in making a martyr of herself and attracting letters of support from "England, France, Jersey and elsewhere". Indeed, she had enough well-wishers to present her with a silver casket containing five £50 notes with which to pay the £250 fine.

Nevertheless, by June 1894 Duchess Mary Caroline was willing to compromise and relinquish all claim on the 3rd duke's personal estate, so long as she was paid £500,000 in cash. As her stepson believed at the outset of the case that the duchess stood to gain £1,500,000, he was content to get away with paying only a third of that amount. This enormous sum had to be raised by selling shares, many of them from the London & North Western Railway Company.[32] There was relief bordering on jubilation in the duke's London office that the case had ended: Henry Wright wrote: "I feel like a cock today – you cannot imagine what a weight has been on me the last 5 or 6 years – now all cast off. I hope never to set eyes on the woman again …".[33] Even if a worse blow had been averted, none of the duke's predecessors had been obliged to pay out such a large sum so rapidly and deprive themselves of such a large source of dividend income.

Initially, the Sutherlands continued as if nothing serious had happened: Stafford House was redecorated and lavish receptions held. But Duchess Mary

Caroline's settlement must have dealt a heavy blow, both financial and psychological. At the height of his quarrel with his father, Strath confided to Henry Chaplin, his brother-in-law, that he did not care what happened to his "Old Houses".[34] This *cri de cœur*, expressed in 1891, was to have an almost prophetic significance: by 1905 the duke was beginning to sell them off, starting with Trentham Park, through the grounds of which flowed – or so it had seemed as early as the 1850s – "a common sewer" in the form of the river Trent.[35] In August 1905 Strath decided to close Trentham Hall "as a residence" and offer it to Staffordshire County Council either as a pottery museum or technical college[36] (although he baulked at the idea of turning it into a women's teacher-training college).[37] The offer was not taken up, and so the contents were sold between November 1906 and July 1907, and the house demolished in September 1911.

With the disappearance of Trentham Park, Strath regarded Canada with increasing enthusiasm. He was fired by the idea of acquiring land that had recently been irrigated by the Canadian Pacific Railways Company, keeping some for himself and settling the rest with farmers.

He proceeded to buy unspecified amounts of land at Brooks, east of Calgary in Alberta, where he started building a mansion in May 1911. By the time of his death in July 1913, he was able to bequeath Brooks to his eldest son, and extensive properties in Alberta, British Columbia and Vancouver Island to his wife and other children.[38] In the last years of his life, Strath was notionally turning his back on death-duty-ridden Britain, and looked forward to spending some part of the year in Canada, the country that promised such a bright future. As Lord Esher wrote in his journal (28 March 1912): "Strath is a monomaniac, his head confused by political phantasmagoria, in which he sees England drowned, and wealth and property secure only in the Dominions."[39]

In such a frame of mind, Strath approached his cousin George Leveson-Gower at the Office of Woods, Lands and Forests about the sale of the remainder of the lease to the Crown. His "very stiff" introductory offer of £150,000 proved unacceptable: Leveson-Gower aimed for a figure of between £65,392 and £78,287,[40] but Strath would not go below £100,000, so negotiations came to an end.[41] It fell to Sir William Lever (1851–1925; created Viscount Leverhulme, 1922; *pl. 102*) to purchase Stafford House. As the Sunlight Soap magnate who had expanded from running a grocery business into building factories and an ideal dormitory town at Port Sunlight village, outside Liverpool, he very much represented new money. He owned a substantial but hardly palatial house in Hampstead, and had a curious penchant for buying great London town houses, such as Stafford House and later Grosvenor House, without any intention of occupying them. Lever, an avid collector of English eighteenth-century *objets d'art*,

Plate 102
Sir William Lever, later 1st Viscount Leverhulme (1851–1925). Created Viscount Leverhulme in 1922, Sir William Lever, who made his fortune with Sunlight Soap, was an avid collector of all things eighteenth-century English, and had dreams of creating a museum of this nature at Stafford House. On his insistence, Stafford House was renamed Lancaster House, the name it has kept ever since.

was very much attracted to the idea of "securing [Stafford House] to the Nation as a Museum for British Works of Art, mainly of the 18th century and earlier, for which it is so eminently suitable". Through intermediaries in the form of George Harley, his solicitor, and Howard Frank, founder of Knight, Frank & Rutley, Lever had been in contact with Sir Lewis Harcourt, Bt, formerly First Commissioner of Works, now Secretary of State to the Colonies in the Liberal government of the day, and (ironically) the son of Sir William Harcourt, Bt, the Chancellor who first introduced death duties in 1894.

At a time when the idea of museums dedicated to the history of a particular city was very much in vogue, Harcourt was determined to create the London equivalent of Paris's Musée Carnavalet. This dream was partly realized in 1911, when the new London Museum was housed on a temporary basis at Kensington Palace. Although Lever would have very much preferred a Museum for British Works of Art, he was prepared to acquiesce with the idea of housing "what is known as 'The London Museum', now temporarily in Kensington Palace, in Stafford House". From the outset, Harcourt had been working closely with Lord Esher on the idea of London's Musée Carnavalet. Esher, of course, knew all about Strath's plans to sell the lease of Stafford House, and – although it cannot be proved – he may even have acted as a go-between. In the event, Strath drastically reduced his offer to £60,000, and in November 1912 Sir William Lever purchased the lease in order to present it to the Crown, for what *The Times* referred to as "some [unspecified] national purpose".[42] As Lord Ronald Gower dolefully noted in his diary, "Stafford House has been sold to a Sir W. Lever! another old house gone – Dunrobin I suppose will be sold next or destroyed like Trentham".[43]

However, a mischievous question in Parliament by W. Moore, Unionist Member for North Armagh, nearly wrecked the whole transaction. He implied that a government concession in West Africa (for growing palm oil, the vital ingredient in his soap) was the real aim of Lever's philanthropic gesture.[44] At the time Lever was in the Congo, but on his return at the end of March 1913, he responded to "insinuations and innuendoes" that his motives were "improper and mercenary" by withdrawing the offer.[45] However, once he had been persuaded that the government and Parliament had repudiated Moore's allegations, Lever changed his mind and renewed the offer for Stafford House at the beginning of May.[46] This time, he suggested that it be used to house the collections of the Museum of London and for "the entertainment of distinguished visitors in London". By introducing the latter proposal, Harcourt was able to persuade Lloyd-George to use government money to pay for the removal of objects from Kensington Palace to Stafford House, and the running costs of the London Museum in its new accommodation. Lever's offer was accepted, and possession of the house was taken on 10 July 1913. Because one of the king's titles was Duke of Lancaster and Lever prided himself on being a Lancashire man, he prevailed on the government to change the name of the house to Lancaster House, a move made official on 16 April 1914.[47] The Sutherlands' intentional farewell to the house where Lord Ronald Gower grew up, and which he so loved, was mournfully recorded in his diary: "The Sale of Stafford House is one of the very sad changes that I have lived to see – in which all that one holds most dear and memorable is now either sold or destroyed."[48] As his diaries go up only to 1912, it is not known whether Lord Ronald ever visited the London Museum in its new surroundings – his great-nephew, the 5th duke, did so, only to find it rather a depressing experience. In July 1913 Queen Alexandra wrote to Henry Chaplin, the 4th duke's brother-in-law and the last member of the family to reside there: "I feel most deeply for you, and having to leave dear old Stafford House at this moment too – enough to break one's heart."[49] The duke and duchess had left by 10 June for Dunrobin, where he contracted pleurisy and died on 27 June 1913. There his funeral took place – with pipers lining the route – with ducal pomp and ceremony that would have been inconceivable after 1918. Although no longer the great hostess of Stafford House, but in many ways liberated from the restrictions that it imposed upon her, Duchess Millicent came to be seen as symbolizing what later seemed halcyon days that abruptly ended on 4 August 1914. Indeed, Gerry, 7th Duke of Wellington was to write to her forty years and two world wars later: "I shall never forget the beauty, charm and sparkle which I shall always associate with you and Stafford House in your time. As Talleyrand said, 'Ceux qui n'ont pas connu la vieille cour n'ont connu la douceur de vivre.'"[50]

If Sir Lewis Harcourt and Lord Esher had the vision to create an equivalent of Paris's Musée Carnavalet in London, they could not have had a better founding keeper than Sir Guy Laking, son of Sir Frances Laking, Bart., physician to Queen Victoria, Edward VII and George V, former honorary inspector of armouries at the Wallace Collection and Keeper of the King's Armoury at Windsor Castle.[51] Having failed to secure the post of keeper of the Wallace Collection, he seized the opportunity – unremunerative as it was at the time, with an annual salary of £100 per annum and no pension[52] – to become director of this new museum. An excellent self-publicist, he wrote an article in *The Times* (15 April 1914), published three weeks after the official opening at Stafford House (23 March 1914), in which he urged his readers: "use the time you have, crib and make it up afterwards, or even steal it, but by all means go and judge the London Museum according to what merits it may possess". Such sentiments attracted 82,000 visitors in the first two months, and helped secure him the honour of Companion of the Order of the Bath.

The museum galleries were arranged roughly in a chronological sequence: the Lower Dining Room became the Roman Room, and the East Ante-Room, with Fabrucci's relief commemorating Garibaldi, became the Prehistoric Room. In the Lower Drawing Room, items dating from between AD 600 and 1066 were displayed. The former Green Library became the Gold and Silver Room, and the duke's Library served as the Keeper's Offices. On the first floor, the Picture Gallery was given over to costumes, the South-West Ante-Room covered the period between 1790 and 1830, the State Drawing Room the eighteenth century and the South-West Drawing Room the late seventeenth century. What until recently had served as the duke and duchess's apartments covered from the Tudors to the Commonwealth. The Banqueting Room was now to be called the

Plate 103
Principal Staircase, Lancaster House, photographed from north-east corner, with detail of *St Sebastian Being Led to Martyrdom*. The staircase was executed by Joseph Bramah & Co., and the design for the balustrading is largely derived from Pierre Le Pautre's *Rampes, apuis, et balcons de serrurerie*.

Plate 106
Former Duke's Library, Lancaster
House. This was created between 1834
and 1835, and the bookcases supplied
by Seddon & Armstrong.

Any constitutional changes would require a two-thirds majority. This conference might be said to have drawn a line under Lancaster House's involvement with southern Africa. This involvement had also included Dr David Livingstone's visit to Stafford House in the 1850s, the anti-slavery conferences of the 1870s and the Boer generals in "provincial suits" gracing Duchess Millicent's soirées. If Stafford House was synonymous with the anti-slavery movement for much of the nineteenth century, the term 'Lancaster House' would be liberally applied to conferences to settle the unhappy aftermath of Britain's imperial past, be it in Zimbabwe, Namibia or Ireland, after the conference of 1979.

Lancaster House still caters for both Foreign Office conferences and government hospitality. Today, gatherings range from London Fashion Week shows, where Tony and Cherie Blair have been hailed as the "most stylish" couple to grace 10 Downing Street (past parallels proving somewhat elusive), to 'bonding sessions' for junior ministers. It remains to be seen whether the Councils of the Isles, meetings that include Britain, Eire, Northern Ireland and the Channel Islands, will satisfy the aspirations of the Ulster Unionists and Irish Nationalists. Britain's membership of the EU and obligations to host European Councils of Ministers at regular intervals have resulted in a rash of temporary structures, mostly in the form of interpreters' booths, the most recent being placed at the west end of the Long Gallery in December 1997. With echoes of the post-war European Advisory Committees, Lancaster House has hosted top-level conferences for NATO, on matters ranging from perestroika to Bosnia and later Kosovo. Indeed, it was at Lancaster House that divergences of opinion on the future of NATO between Margaret Thatcher and Helmut Kohl became wider, the former maintaining a more cautious attitude while Kohl believed in more generous aid to prop up the Gorbachev régime. Kohl had every reason to think it his day of triumph, as the conference was very much going his way. Perhaps he would have felt this more had he known of that unhappy Lancaster House summit nearly seventy years earlier when Lloyd-George laid down his draconian terms for the settling of Germany's war reparations, including the Allies' proposal to seize customs houses around the area where Kohl grew up.

At the same time, Lancaster House boasts wine in its cellars to rival those of the quai d'Orsay, and both food and wine play their parts as diplomatic weapons. Gone are the days when the *Evening News* could make jibes about "Ministry of Works sherry" being served in the newly restored interiors. Brigadier Alan Cowen, chairman of government hospitality from 1980 until 1993, may have insisted on "no bloody fiddly bits on the lemons" but he also toured châteaux and vineyards every summer, building up a virtually unparalleled collection of wines, and discussing menus and *placements* with the Prime Minister of the day. Statesmen shall not, however, live by canapés alone: in the final analysis, the interiors of Lancaster House never cease to impress. President Mittérand of France is reputed to have been rapt in wonder at his first sight of the Principal Staircase. However pressing Margaret Thatcher regarded their agenda, M. Le Président wanted to savour that moment to the full and would not be hurried. This small incident lends credence at least to James Loch's statement about the Principal Staircase being the "finest of its sort in Europe".

In the course of the twentieth century, Lancaster House assumed an identity in which even Duchess Harriet, *la grande duchesse*, could have taken pride. Under the charismatic directorships of both Sir Guy Laking and later Sir Mortimer Wheeler, it triumphantly fulfilled the role of London's Musée Carnavalet. As a centre for high-level conferences and government hospitality, Lancaster House

Plate 107
Signing of the Lancaster House
Agreement in the Long Gallery of
Lancaster House, 21 December 1979.
What is now called the Long Gallery
often serves as an international
conference room. Left (fifth furthest
from the camera) to right: Bishop
Abel Muzorewa, The Rt Hon. Lord
Carrington, The Rt Hon. David
Gilmour, Joshua Nkomo, Robert
Mugabe. In the audience are the
Rt Hon. Margaret Thatcher and
the Rt Hon. Francis Pym.

has witnessed its share of events that have shaped the history of the world since
1945. Its splendid interiors have dazzled many a VIP – even the president of a
country that can boast Versailles in its *patrimoine national* – and it fulfills its role
as Britain's shop window in the world of foreign statesmen and diplomats better
than any other venue. In its way it is continuing the rôle that it played in the
preceding century, although with conferences and receptions rather than
glittering soirées and balls where the visiting head of state might lead off the
dancing with the hostess.

Conclusion

As the twenty-first century dawns, precious few London town houses remain standing, and only one is still occupied (at least in part) by the family that historically owned it, namely Apsley House. Promoted as no. 1, London, Apsley House contains the Wellington Museum. Like Spencer House in St James's, it has been restored to its former glory, and can give visitors at least some idea of what a London town house would have been like in its heyday. Bridgewater House has been mentioned in the introduction in connection with *Brideshead Revisited*. Home House, which until recently housed the Courtauld Institute, is now a club, as is Lansdowne House, although the latter was severely gutted during the 1930s. Nevertheless, the hefty losses make gloomy reading. As early as 1874 Northumberland House had been demolished in order to make way for Northumberland Avenue. The 1920s and 1930s saw the demolition of Grosvenor House, Devonshire House, Norfolk House, Dorchester House and countless others. Just before Londonderry House's turn came in 1962, the last ball to be held there had music supplied by a then relatively obscure band by the name of the Rolling Stones (one can only speculate as to how Lord Ronald Gower or Sir William Rothenstein would have recorded the event).

Stafford House, once the flagship of London town houses, proudly continues that rôle, in the guise of Lancaster House, amid such buildings as still survive. But if we were to play devil's advocate, we might naturally ask whether it really was a "palace", as Queen Victoria described it, or just one of a number of grand town houses. Were others inspired to erect similar buildings in emulation, or did it stand in some sort of glorious architectural isolation? Leaving aside the bricks-and-mortar factor, did Stafford House have as large a household as its rivals? Were the parties there grander, and were they more frequently attended by royalty? Politics and charity help enhance the prestige of a town house, but did Stafford House excel in either sphere?

Queen Victoria's comment should of course be taken as a humorous compliment. Stafford House was originally conceived as the residence of the heir apparent to,

Plate 108
HENRY HOWARD RA (1769–1847), *The Solar System* (1834–36), in the ceiling of the former South-West Drawing Room (also known as the Green Velvet Room). Howard was paid 800 guineas (£840) for his decorations in June 1837.

177

but not the occupant of, the throne. There were no audience, presence or council chambers, and no throne room, unlike, for example, at Buckingham Palace or Carlton House. Nevertheless, Stafford House was far more than just one of a number. First, what was then called York House was free-standing, with "perfect fronts" flanked by terraces, as the *Literary Gazette* observed: such features were unheard of in a town house by the 1820s, and only possible in this case because the house stood on Crown property. In addition, the visual impact on entering Stafford (or Lancaster) House was, and still is, truly palatial. Although fine staircases leading to the *piano nobile* were by no means unprecedented – viz. Home or Northumberland House – none are as imposing as that of Lancaster House. Despite the presence of Canova's *Napoleon Colossus*, that of Apsley House is quite modest in comparison. But then the childless Duke of York and (to a certain extent) the Marquis of Stafford, whose adult children by then had their own residences, had little need to worry about those disadvantages referred to by *Truth* in 1912, namely that "domestic comfort was sacrificed to the entertaining rooms". Dignity and status were all important. Thirdly, with the possible exception of Northumberland House, no other house had what were in effect state apartments on both the ground and first floors. Although the 1839 and 1856 inventories of Stafford House refer to the State Dining Room and the State Drawing Room as being on the first floor, the ground-floor rooms along the south elevation continued to perform the stately function long after the 1st duke's death: it was in the ground-floor Dining Room that Harriet Beecher Stowe took luncheon in 1853; in the adjoining room in 1883 Gladstone made his ceremonial speech on the occasion of the unveiling of a marble roundel of Garibaldi in front of Italian dignitaries; and right up to 1911 the ground-floor Drawing Room was often used as a supper room when balls were held, while dancing took place mostly in the Picture Gallery and Banqueting Room on the first floor. In contrast, the state apartments of the other town houses were confined to either one or other floor: those of Grosvenor House were on the ground floor, whereas those of most others, such as Bridgewater, Montagu and Dorchester Houses, were on the first. It therefore becomes evident that no town house surpassed Stafford House in scale and that Queen Victoria was speaking 'many a true word in jest'.

No architect could fail to be aware of Stafford House, but did it create a precedent that he would be virtually compelled to imitate if he wanted to secure a rich client? Benjamin and Philip Wyatt certainly had sufficient talent, taste and connections, but they lacked the professional and financial competence of a Sir Robert Smirke to prosper over a sustained period. Furthermore, they never published engravings of their more prestigious works or even a collection of designs. Therefore, even if they could both claim to have introduced a style to

Great Britain a good ten years before it was adopted on the Continent, such an omission left the field open for more commercially minded engravers such as Thomas King or C.F. Bielefeld, whose publication *On the use of the Improved Papier Mâché* ... (London 1850) effectively brought Louis XIV out of the town house into the railway hotel.

Nevertheless, one should not confuse the reputation of the Wyatts, beset with dwindling patronage during their latter years, with that of their *chef d'œuvre*, Stafford House. Even if it was never copied slavishly by others, such a massive edifice could never have been far from the minds of architects or clients about to embark on a building in the French style. What greater professional compliment (albeit posthumous) than to have Empress Eugénie of France seriously consider building her own copy of Stafford House? Barry's use of a grand, scagliola-embellished staircase in such an important commission as the Reform Club must surely be seen in part as a compliment to the Wyatts' Principal Staircase. William Burn may have given Montagu House (1853–59) a French Renaissance exterior, but Louis XIV played an important role inside. When Samuel Whitfield Daukes undertook alterations at Dudley House for the 11th Baron Ward, he applied Louis XIV elements to the picture gallery and the ballroom: he even combined French elements in the latter with a heavily coffered, classical ceiling, in a spirit similar to that of Benjamin Wyatt in the Great South Drawing Room at Stafford House. However, neither Burns nor Daukes are known to have made a study of Stafford House, and both could easily have borrowed ornaments from French engravings of the seventeenth and eighteenth centuries, much as Earl de Grey had done, without necessarily having to refer to the Wyatts. But it is doubtful whether they would have considered the use of such a style had the Wyatts not applied it to such great effect at Stafford, Apsley and Londonderry Houses.

But what of the layout of Stafford House? Was it particularly innovative? Its plan can be summarized as a covered central atrium or saloon, some sixty feet by forty, created by the staircase, around which the rooms on all four sides form an outer perimeter. Earlier town houses such as Norfolk or Grosvenor House had centrally placed staircases, but none made such a huge feature of them. Lord Ronald Gower may have praised such an arrangement as being "equally magnificent and commodious".[1] But William Gladstone observed more shrewdly: "the magnificence of the fittings of the house is extraordinary: the staircase most noble: but the rooms appear narrow after it."[2]

In 1842 Thomas Cundy the Younger drew up similar plans for Grosvenor House, but the Marquis of Westminster never used them.[3] Barry produced a fairly similar layout for Bridgewater House, but he intended something more like the courtyard or *cortile* (albeit covered) of an Italian *palazzo*. Indeed, the staircase is tucked away to the eastern side of the building, and hardly the feature that it is at Stafford House. Robert Stayner Holford made his Italianate staircase a central feature of Dorchester House, around which he placed a dining room, ball room and two drawing rooms on the upper floor. Similar arrangements were used at Dudley House and Montagu House (at Whitehall Gardens). But none of these made quite the feature of their main staircases that Wyatt did at Stafford House, nor did they take up more space than state rooms such as galleries, drawing rooms or dining rooms.

A town house with a dominant saloon and staircase could not fail to impress, but it needed space, an increasingly rare commodity as the nineteenth century drew to its end, even in Park Lane or St James's. Not even the fabulously rich Barney Barnato, when he came to build his mansion at 25 Park Lane, adopted any similar layout.[4] As his space was limited to an irregular plot of land where Park Lane and Great Stanhope Street converged, he expanded four floors upwards, so as to accommodate his gallery, billiard room, ballroom, drawing rooms, minstrel's gallery, nursery, servants' quarters and so on. Sir Ernest Cassell's hall and marble staircase at Brook House, Park Lane, was so huge that wags dubbed it "the Giants' Lavatory",[5] but even here the Stafford House atrium arrangement was avoided. In fact, by the 1880s such a layout was becoming obsolete: Stafford House stands in glorious isolation, admired but not copied, lavishly yet tastefully embellished, but hard to imitate without descending into vulgarity.

If we concede that Stafford House was the grandest building of its type, was it in any way a political nerve centre? For all the controversy surrounding Garibaldi's visit, and for all the enthusiasm with which the 2nd duchess embraced the anti-slavery cause, Stafford House was by no means the most political mansion in London. Indeed, until the beginning of the twentieth century it could be described as being somewhat above politics. Those hoping to further their political careers would have had to look elsewhere. The opponents of Home Rule for Ireland would have gravitated towards Devonshire House, whereas Crewe House was the gathering place of the Liberal party in the years leading up to the First World War. In the aftermath, Londonderry House performed that role – and with far greater gusto than Stafford House had done in the 1900s – for the Conservative party and later the National Government. But then, the Conservative and Unionist party had spent most of the decade leading up to 1914 in opposition, whereas it became the party most often in power between 1922 and 1939. Unlike Londonderry House or Cliveden, Stafford House could not really boast of its own political 'set'.

Stafford House was probably foremost in promoting the various charitable causes adopted by society during the nineteenth century. However, it could claim no moral monopoly: Bridgewater House hosted its eponymous committee on "Distress in Lancashire" during the 1860s; Devonshire House held exhibitions and sales on behalf of the Irish Distressed Ladies Fund, and (like Stafford House) a concert in aid of the Royal Normal College and Academy of Music for the Blind; likewise Grosvenor House, which could probably claim second place to Stafford House in this particular context, also hosted events for children's hospitals, various missions and churches, and Armenian relief, not to mention the arts, in the form of the Royal School for Art Needlework.

Because Stafford House was by and large free of political intrigue, the Royal Family could pay frequent visits without being identified with any particular party. However, the Sutherlands enjoyed no exclusive monopoly in entertaining royalty. In June 1849 the queen was entertained at Grosvenor House, where "... the windows in the rear of the mansion being opened discovered a brilliant illumination in the gardens ... [and] the Queen expressed her extreme gratitude at the beautiful effect produced".[6] During the last decade of the Duke of Wellington's life, the Prince Consort regularly attended the annual Waterloo Banquets at Apsley House. The 4th Earl Spencer gave a ball for the queen at Spencer House on 13 July 1857, which was attended by the King of Belgium, Prince Friedrich Wilhelm of Prussia and a host of foreign ambassadors. On 27 May 1851 Charles Dickens staged at Devonshire House an amateur production of Bulwer-Lytton's comedy *Not So Bad as We Seem* in front of the queen and Prince Consort. However, it was at their country seats that other dukes seem mostly to have entertained the royal couple. For example, the Norfolks received them at Arundel Castle in 1846, the Bedfords at Woburn Abbey in 1841 and the 'Bachelor Duke' of Devonshire at Chatsworth in 1843. Visits by the queen and Prince Consort to other town houses were rare, and certainly in the early years of her reign those to Stafford House were fairly frequent.

Soon after she was widowed, the queen, for some unaccountable reason, excluded Stafford House from a notional list of town houses (viz. Grosvenor House, Apsley House and Spencer House, "and not to *all* of these in the *same* year") that the Prince of Wales could visit with her blessing.[7] But the Prince and Princess of Wales were not content with such social restrictions. They happily frequented Stafford House, but they also attended receptions and banquets at Devonshire, Bridgewater and Grosvenor House, not to mention Northumberland House, where a ball was held in July 1873, a mere twelve months before its demolition. In the eyes of posterity, perhaps the greatest town-house reception to be attended by the Prince and Princess of Wales was the costume ball at Devonshire House in celebration of Queen Victoria's Diamond Jubilee. (The Prince of Wales came as the Grand Prior of the Order of St John and the Princess as Marguerite de Valois.) Nevertheless, Stafford House surpassed all others when it came to entertaining royalty: the coronation ball in honour of George V at Stafford House was surely the grand finale of the great town-house receptions.

Running a house of this size and laying on such entertainments would have demanded a large number of servants. At its zenith, Stafford House could boast – according to Loch's survey[8] – a total of fifty-two household and fifteen stable employees, whereas Bridgewater House and Lord Carlisle's establishment at 12 Grosvenor Place had less than half that number. From the census returns of 1861, we learn that Norfolk House was occupied on that day by the Dowager Duchess of Norfolk, her two sons (including the 15th duke in his minority), six daughters and thirty-five servants. Likewise, Dorchester House must have had its full complement: in addition to Robert Stayner Holford, his wife, infant son and three daughters, there were thirty-eight household and six stable servants. Norfolk House had a French nurse and valet, Dorchester House a cook and lady's maid from Paris, and Lansdowne House a French cook and an Italian confectioner. However, the Sutherlands employed more foreign servants – ranging in origin from the West Indies to Poland – than any other large household. Furthermore, a town house with over fifty servants in its employ must have been virtually unique: only Stafford House could boast of such an establishment.

Until the early years of the reign of George V, Stafford House could boast almost all the superlatives associated with town houses. True, it was not necessarily the most political house, and not as great a palace of art as Bridgewater or Grosvenor House. Nevertheless, its magnificence inspired new money, in the form of Sir William Lever, to rescue it. Lever, with his love of the eighteenth century in England and subsequent wish to create a museum dedicated to this period, may well have had in mind the Trentham Romneys that dominated the Picture Gallery from the 1900s onwards. In the event, all these factors must have made Stafford House, in Lever's view, "so eminently suitable", even if it was not used quite as he had first intended. But it was these superlatives, so attractive to Lever, that drove the 4th Duke of Sutherland to abandon Stafford House as early as 1912. Town houses could survive only with huge and ever-harder-to-maintain households to run them. They served their purpose as long as formality and deference dominated; as long as the owners and their circle of friends and acquaintances (particularly the more dynamic among them) preferred balls such as Tsar Alexander II would have attended to those displays of Parisian Apache dancing that Sir William Rothenstein and Lord Ronald Gower found so distasteful, but which others thought exciting and avant-garde. However, in the years leading up to the First World War – and to a far greater extent afterwards – such a building as Stafford House was increasingly thought more suitable as a museum than as a private residence – an almost universal view of all large residences, in town and country alike, for most of the twentieth century (indeed, as early as 1906 the 4th duke had hoped that Trentham Park might be saved if it could be used as a pottery museum).

Would Stafford House have been demolished or had its interiors gutted if Sir William Lever had not stepped in? Probably the fact that it was Crown property, close to Clarence House and St James's Palace, made it far less likely to be pulled down and replaced by a block of flats or offices. (But then, George V had considered demolishing Kensington Palace after the First World War.) What might have happened to Benjamin Dean Wyatt's Louis XIV interiors invites grim speculation. However, depressing as the 5th Duke of Sutherland may have found serried rows of museum display cases in those lavishly gilded rooms where he grew up, even they contributed to the survival of Stafford House and its interiors. The popularity of the London Museum during this period enabled the building to be loved by the general public and appreciated by politicians who would otherwise have been ill-disposed to a system that had allowed town houses to exist in the first place. The fact that Lancaster House, although damaged, was spared the worst of the Blitz and became a much sought-after Foreign Office conference centre after the Second World War meant that it was restored and remained standing until the time when an embarrassing anachronism became a subject of keen historic interest.

Lancaster House or Stafford House? Back in 1953, Christopher Hussey wrote:

> Regrettable in many respects as was the expiry of the London Museum's lease, it is unquestionable that these magnificent rooms can only now be seen and appreciated as they deserve. And now that the circumstances which led to the change of the building's name have ceased to apply, why should not Lancaster House revert to its proper and historic designation as Stafford House?[9]

Such sentiments instantly strike a chord with anyone who has studied and grown to love this building. However, but for the generosity of Sir William Lever, later Lord Leverhulme, the greatest town house of all could have gone the way of so many others. Not even Duchess Millicent, for all her charisma and energy, could have saved it – such a task could only have been achieved by a self-made man with a philanthropic disposition. It was his express wish that Stafford House should be renamed Lancaster House: ultimately, gratitude should prevail over romanticism, and the great pioneering architectural historian Christopher Hussey should – if somewhat hesitantly – be gainsaid, and Leverhulme's wishes be respected.

Notes, Select Bibliography & Picture Credits

Abbreviations used in notes:
BCMR Belvoir Castle Muniment Room, Leicestershire
BCRO Bedfordshire County Record Office, Bedford
BL British Library, London
CA Christie's Archives, London
CHA Castle Howard Archives, Yorkshire
DCMR Dunrobin Castle Muniment Room, Sutherland
DCRO Durham County Record Office, Durham
EP Esher Papers, Churchill College Archives, Cambridge
GHA Goldsmiths' Hall Archives, London
MCCA Messrs Coutts & Co. Archives, London
NAL National Art Library, London
NLOS National Library of Scotland, Edinburgh
PR Probate Register, London
PRO Public Record Office, London
ROTHS. Rothschild Archives, London
RIBA Royal Institute of British Architects, London
SCRO Staffordshire County Record Office, Stafford
SRO Scottish Record Office, Edinburgh
WCRA Windsor Castle Royal Archives
WM Wellington Museum, London

Introduction

1 LORD RONALD GOWER FSA, *My Reminiscences*, 2 vols., London (Kegan Paul) 1883, I, p. 6.

Chapter 1

1 FRANCIS BAMFORD and the DUKE OF WELLINGTON (eds.), *The Journal of Mrs Arbuthnot, 1820–1832*, 2 vols., London (Macmillan) 1950, I, p. 407.
2 BCMR, case 5, shelf 6, no. 12, Castle Building Accounts, 1801–16.
3 JOHN MARTIN ROBINSON, *The Wyatts: An Architectural Dynasty*, intro. by Woodrow Wyatt, Oxford (Oxford University Press) 1974, pp. 90–123.
4 PRO, Crest 2/597, 28 September 1807.
5 Parliamentary Papers III (1841 (I)), 12 May 1841, pp. 543–58.
6 PRO, Crest 2/597, Duke of York to Lords of the Treasury, 23 July 1823.
7 BCMR, case 1, shelf 2, no. 4, Duchess of Rutland to Colonel F.W. Trench, 28 January 1824.
8 ROTHS., VI/10/11, fol. 195.
9 BAMFORD and WELLINGTON 1950, I, p. 385.
10 WCRA, Geo. Addl. MSS 6/75, Samuel Baker & Sons to the Executors of His Royal Highness the late Duke of York, 23 February 1827.
11 H. COLVIN, 'The Architects of Stafford House', *Architectural History*, i, 1958, pp. 17–30, pls. 1a, 1b, 2.
12 *Ibid.*, pl. 2.
13 RIBA, J11/30/2, 3.
14 SCRO, D593/E/7/19, *In the Common Pleas Between Benjamin Dean Wyatt Plt and The Most Noble George Granville Duke of Sutherland Defendant ...*, 8 November 1839, p. 57.
15 BCMR, case 20, shelf 4, no. 9, Sir Herbert Taylor to Colonel F.W. Trench, n.d.
16 J. WATKINS, *The Duke of York: A Biographical Memoir*, London (Fisher) 1827, p. 529.
17 PRO, Works 19/19/1, ff. 68–78, Benjamin Wyatt to Colonel Benjamin Stephenson, 26 August 1825.
18 BCMR, case 20, shelf 5, no. 9, Benjamin Wyatt to the Duchess of Rutland, 18 September 1825.
19 *Ibid.*, Benjamin Wyatt to the Duchess of Rutland, 3 October 1825, 12 October 1825.
20 *Ibid.*, Benjamin Wyatt to the Duchess of Rutland, 6 November 1825.

21 RACHEL LEIGHTON (ed.), *Correspondence of Charlotte Grenville, Lady Williams Wynn and her three sons*, London (Murray) 1920, p. 337.
22 Bamford and Wellington 1950, II, p. 54; BCMR, case 20, shelf 5, no. 11, Duke of York to the Duke of Rutland, 7 December 1826.
23 SCRO: D593/E/7/19, cross-examination of Henry Harrison, December 1841.
24 WCRA, Geo. Addl. MSS 6/32, 6/51.
25 WCRA, Geo. Addl. MSS 6/121, *List of Articles prepared, in Scagliola, for His Royal Highness the late Duke of York and now proposed to be purchased by the Marquis of Stafford*, 13 August 1828.
26 PRO, Crest 35/2431, Benjamin Wyatt to Alexander Milne, 13 November 1828.
27 J. HARRIS, "C.R. Cockerell's "Ichnographica Domestica"', *Architectural History*, xiv, 1971, pp. 20–21. C.R. Cockerell (diary, following 15 December 1826).
28 WCRA, Geo. Addl. MSS 6/32, 51.
29 MCCA, Archives, Duke of York Bank Account, 14 January – 2 June 1826.
30 PRO, Crest 35/2429: *The Comm'rs of H.M.'s Woods & an account with the Excrs of HRH the Late Duke of York – Jan 7 1835*.
31 PRO, Crest 35/2429, Charles Gower and James Howard to the Lords of the Treasury, 27 March 1857.
32 *Ibid.*
33 Bamford and WELLINGTON 1950, II, p. 28.
34 J. PREBBLE, *The Highland Clearances*, London (Secker & Warburg) 1963, p. 53; E. Richards, *The Leviathan of Wealth*, London (Routledge & Kegan Paul) 1973, p. 289.
35 BL, BL Addl. MS 40, 387, ff. 205, 17 June 1826.
36 E. BERESFORD CHANCELLOR, *The Private Palaces of London*, London (Kegan Paul) 1908, p. 349; DUKE OF SUTHERLAND, *The Story of Stafford House*, London (Bless) 1935, pp. 2–3; DUKE OF BUCKINGHAM and CHANDOS, KG, *Memoirs of the Court of George IV 1820–1830*, London (Longman, Green & Co.) 1870, II, pp. 246–47, p. 364.
37 BL, Addl. MS 40, 387, ff. 205.
38 SCRO, D593/E/7/14, *Between Henry Burnell Plt and Arthur Duke of Wellington, George Granville Leveson Gower, Marquess of Stafford, Sir Herbert Taylor, Benjamin Charles Stephenson ... defendants*, 11 January 1833, p. 5.
39 PRO, C13/2215, *Burnell v. Taylor*, 24 July 1828.
40 SCRO, D593/E/7/14, *Between Henry Burnell*

Plt and Arthur Duke of Wellington, George Granville Leveson Gower, Marquess of Stafford, Sir Herbert Taylor, Benjamin Charles Stevenson ... defendants, 11 January 1833, p. 4.
41 SCRO, D593/K/1/5/24, James Loch to Edward Gatty, 16 November 1828; D593/K/1/3/19, W. Loftus Lowndes to Edward Gatty, 14 October 1831.
42 PRO, C13/2215, *Burnell v. Taylor*.
43 PRO, C33/864, 31 July 1834; SCRO, D593/K/1/3/24, Edward Gatty to James Loch, 27 January 1836.
44 'A Bill to enable Her Majesty's Commissioners of Woods ... to complete the Contract for the Sale of York House, and to purchase certain Lands for a Royal Park', *Parliamentary Papers*, III (1841 (I)), pp. 543–58; SCRO, D593/K/1/3/29, Lord Duncannon to James Loch, 21 April 1841.
45 SCRO, D593/K/1/3/30, Alexander Milne to James Loch, 26 February 1841; Alexander Milne to James Loch, 31 March 1841.
46 SCRO, D593/E/7/19, *In the Common Pleas ...*, 8 November 1839, p. 7.
47 *The Gentleman's Magazine*, XCVII, January to June 1827, p. 82.
48 *The Debts of his Royal Highness the Duke of York*, London 1832, *passim*.
49 WCRA, Geo. Addl. MSS 6/101.
50 PRO, Crest 35/2426.
51 PRO, C13/2215, *Burnell v. Taylor*.
52 BL Addl. MS 40387, ff. 198–99, Colonel Benjamin Stephenson to Sir Robert Peel, 19 June 1826.
53 *Parliamentary Papers*, XIV (1833). Appendix 5, pp. 192–95.
54 PREBBLE 1963; ERIC RICHARDS, *A History of the Highland Clearances*, 2 vols., London (Croom Helm) 1982–85.
55 NLOS, Dep. 313/827, Earl Gower to Lady Stafford, 16 June 1827.
56 NLOS, Dep. 313/827, Earl Gower to Lady Stafford, 13 June 1827.
57 NLOS, Dep. 313/827, Earl Gower to Lady Stafford, 18 June 1827.
58 NLOS, Dep. 313/827, Earl Gower to Lady Stafford, 25 June 1825.
59 NLOS, Dep. 313/827, Earl Gower to Lady Stafford, 2 July 1827.
60 *Ibid.*
61 SRO, GD268/219/35, Lady Stafford to James Loch, 23 July 1827.
62 SRO, GD268/219/36, Lady Stafford to James Loch, 11 July 1827.
63 NLOS, Dep. 313/827, Lord Gower to Lady Stafford, Sunday 18 July 1827.

64 SCRO, D593/N/6/2, *Queries to be submitted to the Marquis of Stafford relative to the completion of York House*, 16 February 1828.

65 SCRO, D593/K/1/3/16, Benjamin Wyatt to James Loch, 16 February 1828.

66 SRO, GD268/219/35, Lady Stafford to James Loch, n.d., c. July 1827.

67 SCRO, D593/K/1/5/24, Benjamin Wyatt to James Loch, 1 September 1828.

68 SCRO, D593/K/1/3/16, Benjamin Wyatt to James Loch, 17 December 1828.

69 SCRO, D593/K/1/3/17, Benjamin Wyatt to James Loch, 18 February 1829.

70 SCRO, D593/K/1/5/25, James Loch to Lord Stafford, 12 April 1829.

71 SRO, GD268/221/35, Lady Stafford to James Loch, 18 August 1829.

72 SRO, GD 268/221/24, Lady Sutherland to James Loch, 24 August 1829.

73 SCRO, D593/N/6/5, building admeasurements, November 1828 – March 1829.

74 SCRO, D593/N/6/6, building admeasurements, April – August 1829.

75 SCRO, D593/R/2/10/6.

76 GEOFFREY DE BELLAIGUE and PAT KIRKHAM, 'George IV and the Furnishing of Windsor Castle', *Furniture History*, VIII, 1972, pp. 1–34; JAMES YORKE, "The Furnishing of Stafford House by Nicholas Morel 1828–1830", *Furniture History*, XXXII, 1996, pp. 46–80.

77 SCRO, D593/N/6/3, June 1828, £575.8s. 3½d.; D593/N/6/4, October 1828, £1073. 8s. ½d.; D593/N/6/5, March 1829, £5360. 19s. 3½d.

78 David Roberts to D.R. Hay, 10 July 1830; David Roberts to D.R. Hay, 24 September 1832. (I am very grateful to Helen Guiterman for sending me a transcript of these two letters.)

79 SCRO, D593/N/6/5.

80 SCRO, D593/K/1/3/17, Benjamin Wyatt to James Loch, 5 February 1829.

81 SCRO, D593 K/1/5/25, James Loch to Benjamin Wyatt, 25 June 1829.

82 SRO, GD268/221/34, Lady Stafford to James Loch, 24 August 1829.

83 SCRO, D593/K/3/21, Benjamin Wyatt to James Loch, 27 July 1833 and 31 July 1833.

84 SCRO, D593, P22/1/16 (1), Benjamin Wyatt to the Duke of Sutherland, 1 August 1833.

85 NLOS, Dep. 313/836, Thomas Grenville to the Duke of Sutherland, 25 September 1833.

86 SCRO, D593/K/1/5/29, James Loch to George Rennie, 4 October 1833.

87 SCRO, D593/K/1/3/31, George Rennie to James Loch, 4 October 1833.

88 NLOS, Dep. 313/827, Earl Gower to Lady Stafford, 13 June 1827.

89 D593/P/22/1/16 (11), Duke of Sutherland to Benjamin Wyatt , 23 October 1833.

90 SCRO, D593/P22/1/16 (12), Benjamin Wyatt to the Duke of Sutherland, 23 October 1833.

91 SCRO, D593/P22/1/16 (15), Benjamin Wyatt to the Duke of Sutherland, 4 November 1833.

92 SCRO, D593/E/7/19, note, Duke of Sutherland, n.d. [(?) November 1839]

93 SCRO, GD268/363/31, Sir Robert Smirke to the Duke of Sutherland, 19 November 1833.

94 SCRO, D593/K/1/3/22, Sir Robert Smirke to James Loch, 15 December 1834.

95 PRO, Crest 2/597, *16 May 1834. Stafford House Archt's report on the Duke of Sutherland's appl. for sanction to the building of detached kitchen offices 16 May 1834.*

96 SCRO, D593/P22/1/16 (6), Duke of Sutherland to Benjamin Wyatt, 28 September 1833.

97 SCRO, D593/R/7/15, inventory of Stafford House, 1839.

98 SCRO, D593/P22/1/16 (21), Benjamin Wyatt to the Duke of Sutherland, 12 March 1834.

99 SCRO, GD268/364/5, Duke of Sutherland to James Loch, 22 June 1834.

100 SCRO, D593/K/1/5/30, James Loch to the Duke of Sutherland, 17 December 1834.

101 *Ibid.*

102 JOHN CORNFORTH, 'Stafford House revisited' – part II, *Country Life*, CLXIV, no. 3741, 14 November 1968, p. 1260.

103 SCRO, D593/P22/1/16 (5), Benjamin Wyatt to the Duke of Sutherland, 19 September 1833.

104 SCRO, D593/P22/1/16, Benjamin Wyatt to the Duke of Sutherland, 15 December 1834.

105 SCRO, D593/K/1/3/23, Benjamin Wyatt to John Fish, 12 August 1835.

106 SCRO, D593/P22/1/16 (69), Benjamin Wyatt to George Jackson, 12 February 1836.

107 SCRO, D593/K/1/3/23, Benjamin Wyatt to John Fish, 12 August 1835.

108 SCRO, D593/P22/1/16 (70), Benjamin Wyatt to the Duke of Sutherland, 2 March 1836.

109 SCRO, D593/N/6/1, *Statement of Account ... For Time Employed on various Designs and Drawings for His Grace, connected with works carried on in the additions to, & finishing of, Stafford House,* n.d.

110 SCRO, D593/R/7/15 (1839 inventory); D593/R/7/19 (1856 inventory).

111 SCRO, D593/N/6/10, George Morant & Son, 9 December 1834.

112 SCRO, D593/P22/1/28, Richard Westmacott to the Duke of Sutherland, 5 June 1837; Henry Howard to the Duke of Sutherland, 24 June 1837.

113 WCRA, *Queen Victoria's Journals*, 4 July 1838.

114 SCRO, D593/R/1/26/26C, George Morant & Son, January – December 1836.

115 JAMES YORKE, "Desiré Dellier – 'Arrant Scoundrel'", *Furniture History*, XXXIII, 1997, pp. 259–63.

116 SCRO, D593/R/1/26/26CA, George Morant & Son, January – December 1837.

117 *Art Journal Illustrated Catalogue: The Industry of All Nations*, London (George Virtue) 1851, p. 34.

118 SCRO, D593/R/1/26/26D, George Morant & Son, January – December 1838.

119 SCRO, D593/N/6/2, *Statement of the Payments made on Account of Stafford House &c from the Year 1828 to July 1837.*

120 SCRO, D593/K/1/5/35, James Loch to Charles Barry, 13 September 1839.

121 SCRO, D593/N/6/1, *passim.*

122 SCRO, D593/P22/1/16 (123), James Loch to the Duke of Sutherland, 20 June 1838.

123 SCRO, D593/E/7/19, Duke of Sutherland to James Loch, 13 November 1839.

124 SCRO, D593/E/7/19, *Note of Consultation with Architects at Stafford House,* n.d.

125 SCRO, D593/P22/1/16 (143), James Loch to Benjamin Wyatt, 26 June 1839.

126 SCRO, D593/N/6/1, 10–17 May 1834, p. 32.

127 SCRO, D593/P22/16/1 (87), Benjamin Wyatt to the Duchess of Sutherland, 30 August 1836.

128 SCRO, D593/P22/1/16 (97), Benjamin Wyatt to the Duke of Sutherland, 17 March 1837.

129 LORD RONALD GOWER FSA, Stafford House Letters, London (Kegan Paul) 1891, pp. 217–18.

130 SCRO, D593/P22/1/16, no. 103, Benjamin Wyatt to the Duke of Sutherland, 3 April 1837.

131 SCRO, D593/P22/1/16 (114), Benjamin Wyatt to the Duke of Sutherland, 10 November 1837.

132 NLOS, Dep. 313/831, Thomas Grenville to the Duke of Sutherland, 15 February 1841.

133 SCRO, D593 P22/1/16 (122), Benjamin Wyatt to the Duke of Sutherland, 19 June 1838.

134 SCRO, D593/E/7/19, *In the Court of Common Pleas between Benjamin Dean Wyatt (plaintiff) and the Most Noble George Granville Duke of Sutherland*, January 1840.

135 SRO, GD268/373/29, 33, Duchess of Sutherland to James Loch, n.d.

136 ROBERT STANLEY MORGAN, 'Benjamin Wyatt and his Noble Clients', *Architectural Review*, CLXV, no. 864, February 1969, p. 105.

137 RICHARD EDGCUMBE (ed.), *The Diary of Frances Lady Shelley 1818–1873*, 2 vols., II, London (John Murray) 1913, p. 26.

138 SCRO, D593/K/1/5/29, James Loch to Charles Barry, 26 November 1833.

139 SCRO, D593/K/1/3/21, Charles Barry to James Loch, 4 October 1833.

140 NLOS, Dep. 313/1163, James Loch to the Duke of Sutherland, 1 September 1839.

141 SRO, GD269/370/12, James Loch to the Duchess of Sutherland, 25 September 1838.

142 NLOS, Dep. 313/1163, James Loch to the Duke of Sutherland, 14 January 1838.

143 SCRO, D593/K/1/5/35, James Loch to Charles Barry, 2 April 1839.

144 NLOS, Dep. 313/828, Duke of Sutherland to the Duchess Countess of Sutherland, 28 October 1833.

145 SRO, GD268/368/32–34, Duchess of Sutherland to James Loch, 21 September [(?) 1838].

146 SRO, GD 268/364/1, Duke of Sutherland to James Loch, 22 December 1833.

147 SRO, GD 268/364/19, Duke of Sutherland to James Loch, n.d. [(?) December 1835].

148 SCRO, D593/P22/1/16 (52), Benjamin Wyatt to Sir Robert Smirke, 16 August 1834.

149 NAL, MSL/1996/2, Duke of Sutherland to Benjamin Wyatt, n.d.

150 SCRO, D593/K/1/3/27, May 30 1839, Sir Robert Smirke to James Loch, 30 May 1839.

151 NLOS, Dep. 313/1163, James Loch to the Duke of Sutherland, 1 September 1839.

152 SCRO, D593/N/6/15, 31 December 1839.

153 SCRO, D593/K/1/3/29, Geo Readman to James Loch, 14 December 1841.

154 SCRO, D593/K/1/5/34, James Loch to Charles Barry, 13 September 1839.

155 SCRO, D593/N/6/14, 31 March 1840 to 31 March 1841: total £8185.3s.0d.; D593/N/6/15, 31 March 1841 to 31 December 1841: total £6161.15s.4d.

156 SCRO, D593/K/1/5/34, James Loch to Charles Barry, 13 September 1839.

157 SCRO, D593/E/7/19, *Account of works executed from Drawings by Mr Wyatt between March 1835 and Christmas 1841,* 28 November 1839.

158 SCRO, D593/K/1/3/27, H. Galeazzi to James Loch, 30 March 1839.

159 SCRO, D593/K/1/3/27, Alex Hathorn to James Loch, 16 October 1839, 9 November 1839.

160 SCRO, D593/N/6/14, George Jackson & Son, 30 August 1841; D593/N/6/15, George Jackson & Son, 5 May 1842.

161 SCRO, D593/N/6/1, p. 261.

162 SCRO, D593/N/6/12.

163 SCRO, D593/K/1/3/27, Alex Hathorn to James Loch, 9 November 1839.

164 SCRO, D593/K/1/3/27, Sir Robert Smirke to James Loch, 6 April 1839, 10 April 1839.

165 SCRO, D593/R/2/19/32, John Henning's bill for 27 August 1840.

166 SCRO, D593/N/6/14, Henry Hudson's bill, 1 July 1840; D593/N/6/13 Morant's bill, 1 January 1839 to Lady Day 1840.

167 SCRO, D593/R/2/31/1, *Fish's House Bills,* Christmas 1843.

168 SCRO, D593/K/1/5/45, Alex Hathorn to Charles Barry, 19 April 1844.

169 SCRO, D593/K/I/3/31, Alexander Milne to James Loch, February 1843.

170 SCRO, D593/R/2/31/1, Lady Day 1845.

171 SCRO, D593/K/1/3/37, Duke of Sutherland to James Loch, 15 May 1849; Messrs Drummond to James Loch, 4 July 1849.

172 SCRO, D593/K/1/5/78, James Loch to the Duke of Sutherland, 31 March 1854.

173 SCRO, D593/K/1/3/40, Duchess of Sutherland to James Loch, 3 March 1852.

174 SCRO, D593/K/1/3/40, Duke of Sutherland to James Loch, 25 May 1852; D593/K/1/3/43, Duke of Sutherland to James Loch, 23 January 1855.

175 SCRO, D593/K/1/5/82, James Loch to Messrs Drummonds, 3 February 1855.

176 *Ibid.*, Duke of Sutherland to James Loch, 23 January 1855.

177 SCRO, D593/K/1/5/97, George Loch to the Duchess of Sutherland, 30 December 1857.

178 David Roberts to Henry Bicknell, 15 May 1860 (private collection), quoted in DAVID BLISSET, 'Sir Charles Barry (1795–1860): A Reassessment of his Travels and Early Career', unpublished doctoral dissertation, Oxford Polytechnic, November 1982, pp. 242, 269.

Chapter 2

1 GEORGE SMITH, *Cabinet-Maker's and Upholsterer's Guide*, London 1826, p. 173.

2 PRINCE PÜCKLER-MUSKAU, *A Tour in Germany, Holland and England, in the years 1826, 1827 and 1828*, trans. Sarah Austin, London 1832, IV, pp. 338–39.

3 *Carlton House: The Past Glories of George IV's Palace*, exhib. cat., London, Queen's Gallery, 1991, pp. 120, 123.

4 PHILIP MANSEL, *The Eagle in Splendour*, London (Philip's) 1987, p. 78.

5 EDGCUMBE, *op. cit.*, I, London (John Murray) 1912, p. 110.

6 FRANCES COLLARD, *Regency Furniture*, Woodbridge (Antique Collector's Club) 1985, p. 111, pl. 12.

7 ELIZABETH, DUCHESS OF RUTLAND, *Journal of a Trip to Paris by the Duke and Duchess of Rutland, July MDCCCXIV*, London 1815, pp. 19, 21.

8 *Ibid.*, p. 21.

9 BCMR, case 1, shelf 2, no. 4, Duchess of Rutland to Colonel F.W. Trench, 13 June 1824.

10 BCMR, case 20, shelf 5, no. 4, Matthew Cotes Wyatt to the Duke of Rutland, 28 September 1824.

11 BCMR, case 20, shelf 5, no. 4, Matthew Cotes Wyatt to the Duke of Rutland, October 1825.

12 BCMR, case 20, shelf 5, item 4, Matthew Cotes Wyatt to the Duke of Rutland, n.d.

13 BAMFORD and WELLINGTON 1950, II, p. 230.

14 REVD IRWIN ELLER, *The History of Belvoir Castle from the Norman Conquest to the Nineteenth Century*, London (R. Tyas) 1841, p. 300.

15 M. Christian Baulez, Conservateur des Meubles at the Château de Versailles, suggests that the boiserie may have come from the Hôtel Noailles in the rue St-Honoré, Paris: Mme de Maintenon's niece married into the de Noailles family, hence, perhaps, the attribution.

16 BCMR, case 1, shelf 2, no. 4, Duchess of Rutland to Colonel F.W. Trench, 12 October 1824.

17 SCRO, D593/P/22/1/16(23), Benjamin Wyatt

to the Duke of Sutherland, 14 March 1834.

18 NLOS, Stuart de Rothesay Papers, MS
21313, George Gunn to Lord Stuart de
Rothesay, Paris, 12 January 1834. (I am very
grateful to my colleague, Sarah Medlam,
Victoria and Albert Museum, London, for
allowing me to use her research on this
point.)

19 SCRO, D593/P/22/16/1(5), Benjamin Wyatt
to the Duke of Sutherland, 19 September
1833.

20 DE BELLAIGUE and KIRKHAM 1972.

21 Ibid., p. 4; PRO, LC1/1(4), J.C. Herries to the
Lord Chamberlain, 14 September 1826.

22 A.F. CIRCKET, 'History of Wrest House',
Bedfordshire Historical Record Society (April
1846), LVIX, 1980, pp. 65–87; SIMON
HOUFFE, 'Wrest Park, Bedfordshire' – part
I, Country Life, CXLVII, no. 3818, 25 June
1970, pp. 1250–53, part II, Country Life,
CXLVII, no. 3819, 2 July 1970, pp. 18–21.

23 BCRO, CRT 190/45/2, typescript of journal
in the property of Lord Lucas, p. 45.

24 BCRO, L33/219–24.

25 NLOS, Dep. 313/793, Earl of Ellesmere to
the Duke of Sutherland, 5 January 1853.

26 London, GHA, Committee Book, 1823–37,
no. 1619.B.39, p. 423.

27 Smith 1826, p. 173.

28 Ibid., pp. iv–v.

29 Architectural Magazine, i, 1834, p. 313.

30 SCRO, D593, P22/1/16 (133), Benjamin
Wyatt to the Duke of Sutherland,
14 February 1839.

31 EDGCUMBE, op. cit., II, p. 26.

32 BCMR, case 20, shelf 5, no. 4, Benjamin
Wyatt to the Duchess of Rutland,
22 November 1825.

33 NLOS, Dep. 313/831, 2nd Duke of
Sutherland to the Duchess Countess of
Sutherland, January 1838.

34 SCRO, D593/P/22/1/16(14), Benjamin Wyatt
to the Duke of Sutherland, 28 October 1833.

35 SCRO, D593/P22/1/16(79), Benjamin Wyatt
to the Duke of Sutherland, 29 June 1836.

36 SCRO, D593/P22/1/16(116), Benjamin
Wyatt to the Duke of Sutherland,
10 January 1838.

37 SCRO, D593/P/22/1/16(119), Benjamin Wyatt
to the Duke of Sutherland, 23 February
1838.

38 SCRO, D593/P/22/1/16(62), Benjamin Wyatt
to the Duke of Sutherland, 24 March 1835.
See also D593/P/22/1/16(69), Benjamin
Wyatt to the Duke of Sutherland,
12 February 1836; ibid. (73), Benjamin
Wyatt to the Duke of Sutherland, 28 April 1836;
ibid. (74), Benjamin Wyatt to the Duke of
Sutherland, 2 May 1836.

39 Information supplied by Sir Howard Colvin.

40 SCRO, D593/E/7/19 (6), William Gooding
Coleman Esqre sworn, Examined by Mr
Harrison as follows, p. 22.

41 NLOS, Dep. 313/793, Earl of Ellesmere to
the Duke of Sutherland, 5 January 1853,
9 January 1853: "Let Blondel wait for me on
the side table as you propose ..."

42 Calignani's Paris Guide or, Stranger's
Companion through the French Metropolis,
tenth edition, 1822, p. 433 (I am most
grateful to my colleague Dr C. Sarjentson
for alerting me to this publication); Circket
1980, p. 67.

43 SCRO, D593/E/7/19(6), William Gooding
Coleman Esqre sworn, Examined by Mr
Harrison as follows, p. 18.

44 Ibid., p. 17.

45 DCRO, D/LO/E/772(I).

46 SCRO, D593/R/2/10/6, The Most Noble the
Marquis of Stafford Bought of Morel &
Seddon, Item 62, 30 March 1830.

47 WM, photographs of a selection of bills and
letters at Stratfield Saye (Stratfield Saye

Photographs; Bernasconi's plasterers' bills
for this room, if they have survived, were not
included).

48 SCRO, D593/K/1/3/17, Benjamin Wyatt to
James Loch, 5 February 1829.

49 Bamford and Wellington 1950, II, p. 343.

50 WM, Benjamin Wyatt to the Duke of
Wellington, 7 August 1829 (Stratford Saye
Photographs).

51 BAMFORD and WELLINGTON 1950, II, p. 335.

52 Ibid., II, p. 333.

53 S.S. JERVIS, 'Picture Frames and Picture
Hanging at Apsley House', in C.M.
Kauffmann, Catalogue of Paintings in the
Wellington Museum (Victoria and Albert
Museum) 1982, p. 17.

54 SCRO, D593/N/6/1, 'My own time drawing
sketch of exact sizes and shapes of Ivy leaf
and berry ornament (full size) for pilasters
in South West Drawing Room', 27
December 1834 – 3 January 1835, p. 80.

55 Ibid., 'My own time ... great South Drawing
Room; sketching the Flower in the Octagon
panels in the Ceiling of Do', 20–27 June
1835, p. 134.

56 SCRO, D593/E/7/19(6), p. 11.

57 SCRO, D593/N/6/1, 'Clerk's time ...
Drawing (full size) of circular band in
centre of Dining Room Ceiling ... plan of
intersecting circles in Ceiling of Dining
Room' 13–20 September 1834, p. 56; "Plan
of ... Enrichments of the four Circular
compartments of the Dining Room Ceiling
to contain double SS in each', 4–11 October
1834, p. 59.

58 Ibid., 'Clerk's time ... Drawing of the
Enrichment of the cove of the Great Dining
Room', 7–14 October 1833, p. 2.

59 Ibid., 'Clerks own time ... Sections of Dining
Room with enrichments; – Enrichments in
Panels (full size) for Quadrants of Dining
Room', 17–24 June 1837, p. 261.

60 Ibid., 'Clerk's time ... Drawing (full size) of
Archivolt for recess at West end at Dining
Room ... My own time ... Making out details
of Archivolt (full size) for arched recess at
West end of Dining Room', 17–24 June 1837,
p. 261.

61 SCRO, D593/P/22/1/16(69), Benjamin Wyatt
to the Duke of Sutherland, 12 February
1836.

62 SCRO, D593/N/6/1, 'Clerk's time ... Plan of
North and South ends of Gallery, describing
the intersecting circles in the same ...',
16–23 May 1835, p. 122.

63 Ibid., 'Clerk's time ... Drawing of Pediment
over doors and Glass frames in Gallery',
15–22 August 1835, p. 147.

64 Ibid., 'My own time ... Arranging details for
pannelled [sic] soffits of arched recesses on
west side of Gallery; making out
Enrichments of archivolts & of panels',
p. 49.

65 SCRO, D593/N/6/1, 'Clerks time ... Working
Drawing (full size) of Pilasters above the
Impost in Gallery', 23–30 July 1836, p. 205,
'Clerk's time ... Drawing (full size) of
Enrichment on Molding [sic] of Pannel
above Impost in Gallery...', 30 July –
6 August 1836, p. 207.

66 RIBA, Charles Barry, travel diaries (I
(June–September 1817) and XVII
(June–September 1820) cover periods spent
in Paris).

67 BARRY, op. cit., I, 7 July 1817.

68 Ibid., 24 August 1817.

69 CHARLES BARRY, op. cit., XVII. Pencil notes
written on an unpaginated end paper.

70 SCRO, D593/P22/1/16(3), Benjamin Wyatt
to the Duke of Sutherland, 10 August 1833.

71 Report from the Select Committee on Arts and
Manufactures, London 1836, p. iii.

72 Ibid., p. 46, para. 540.

73 Ibid., p. 46, para. 543.

Chapter 3

1 SCRO, D593/P/26/2/7, press cuttings:
untitled and undated cutout (c. 22 June
1875).

2 HARRIET BEECHER STOWE, Sunny
Memories of Foreign Lands, London
(Sampson & Lowe) 1854, pp. 211, 213.

3 SCRO, D593/R/4/1–8 (1829–75).

4 SCRO, D593/R/4/1, servants' wage book,
1829–32.

5 Ibid.

6 SCRO, D593/R/4/2.

7 SCRO, D593/K/1/3/32, James Loch to
Alexander Hathorne, 8 April 1844. The table
is attached to this letter.

8 See note above; also SCRO, D593/R/2/13/20,
statement of wages from 25 December 1837
to 25 June 1838; D593/R/2/20/21, list of half-
yearly wages up to 25 December 1840;
D593/R/2/25/3 Do. up to June 1844 (etc.);
D593/K/1/3/38, received from Richard
Walker, 25 February 1850.

9 SCRO, D593/K/1/5/25, Thomas Dodsworth,
Memorandum as to Servants, 15 May 1830.

10 SCRO, D593/K/1/3/22, Duke of Sutherland
to the servants, 22 April 1834.

11 SCRO, D593/R/7/15, Stafford House
inventory, 1839.

12 SCRO, D593/K/1/3/15, Michael Gummow to
James Loch, August 1827.

13 SRO, GD268/238/28, James Loch to the
Duke of Sutherland, 24 January 1837.

14 SCRO, D593/R/2/29/4, Barber & Calvert bill
for £264. 16s. od. 9 February 1848.

15 SCRO, D593/K/1/3/32, E. Thurgood to
James Loch, 19 November 1844.

16 SCRO, D593/K/1/3/32, Duchess of
Sutherland to James Loch, n.d.
(c. December 1844); SCRO D593/K/1/3/37,
Duchess of Sutherland to James Loch, n.d.
(c. April 1849); James Loch to the Duchess
of Sutherland, 16 April 1849.

17 SCRO, D593/K/1/3/32, Alexander Hathorn
to James Loch, 8 April 1844; ibid., Marquis
of Zetland to James Loch, n.d. (c. June
1844).

18 SCRO, D593/K/1/3/32, Richard Walker to
James Loch, 8 May 1844.

19 SCRO, D593/K/1/5/51. Richard Walker to
James Loch, 12 February, 19 February 1847.

20 Ibid.

21 SCRO, D593/P/26/2/7, press cuttings:
undated and untitled newspaper cutting:
'Death of the Duke of Sutherland's
Highland Piper – John MacAlister'.

22 STOWE 1854, p. 214.

23 SCRO, D593/K/1/3/50, Dowager Duchess of
Sutherland to George Loch, 19 November
1862.

24 PRO, census microfilm HO107/1481,
fol. 10–11. Census for 1851.

25 Ibid., RG12/214, fol. 40. Census for 1891.

26 SCRO, D593/K/1/7/47, Henry Wright to Mr
Grant, 26 July 1894.

27 SCRO, D593/R/4/4, wage book for 1850–55;
D593/R/4/5, wages book, 1859–61;
D593/R/4/6, wages book, 1870.

28 SCRO, D593/R/4/8, servants' wages book,
1875–79.

29 DCRO, D/LO/F631(6), Henry Chaplin to the
Duke of Sutherland, 18 January 1892.

30 SCRO, D593/Q/2/1/20, Duke of Sutherland
to Henry Wright, 6 November 1892.

31 SCRO, D593/P/30/6, Household Men
Servants as at January 16 1913.

32 SCRO, D593/K/1/5/75, James Loch to
Richard Doridant, 26 April 1853.

33 SCRO, D593/K/1/3/26, L. Vantini to James

Loch, 8 October 1838. D593/R/1/14/1, p. 161.

34 SCRO, D593/K/1/3/28, Thomas Jackson to
James Loch, 9 March 1840.

35 SCRO, D593/K/1/3/28, L. Vantini to James
Loch, 18 January 1851.

36 SCRO, D593/Q/1/1, Duke of Sutherland to
James Loch, 30 March 1844.

37 SCRO, D593/K/1/3/29, Thomas Jackson to
James Loch, 13 January 1841.

38 SCRO, D593/K/15/47, James Loch to the
Duke of Sutherland, 12 May 1845.

39 SCRO, D593/K/1/3/32, untitled and
undated tables of expenditure, included in
the letters for April 1844.

40 SCRO, D593/K/1/5/60, Duchess of
Sutherland to James Loch, 21 February
1849.

41 SCRO, D593/K/1/3/39, Richard Walker to
James Loch, 18 January 1851.

42 SCRO, D593/K/1/5/74, James Loch to the
Duchess of Sutherland, 14 January 1853.

43 SCRO, D593/K/1/3/41, Duchess of
Sutherland to James Loch, February 1853.

44 SCRO, D593/K/1/3/62, John Culverwell to
Henry Wright, 18 August 1875.

45 Ibid., John Whittaker to Henry Wright,
20 September 1875.

46 SCRO, D593/K/1/3/34, Duchess of
Sutherland to James Loch, 7 January 1846.

47 SCRO, D593/K/1/3/34, Duke of Sutherland
to James Loch, 7 January 1846.

48 LORD RONALD GOWER FSA, My
Reminiscences, 2 vols., London (Kegan Paul)
1883, I, p. 379.

49 SCRO, D593/R/2/42/1.

50 SCRO, D593/R/18/1, Duke of Sutherland's
account book, January 1845 – June 1855.

51 DCMR, Lord Ronald Gower's diaries, 28
January 1855.

52 BERNHARD GÄBLER, Die vollständige
Litturgie und die 39 Artikel der Kirche von
England nebst einer einleitung ... von G.G.,
Saxe-Altenberg 1843.

53 DCMR, Lord Ronald Gower's diaries,
13 February 1855.

54 Ibid., 11 April 1857.

55 Ibid., 1 March 1861.

56 5th Duke of Sutherland, Looking Back,
London (Oldham Press) 1957. p. 53.

57 LORD RONALD GOWER FSA, Old Diaries,
1881–1901, London (John Murray) 1902,
p. 386.

58 SCRO, D593/P/22/1/32, Duchess Harriet to
the 2nd Duke of Sutherland, 27 July 1845.

59 DCMR, Lord Ronald Gower's diaries,
26 November 1888.

60 WCRA, Queen Victoria's journals, 27
November 1888, p. 139.

61 SCRO, D593/R/2/31/2, bills for midsummer
1852; D593/K/1/3/40, John Culverwell to
James Loch, 19 November 1852.

62 SCRO, D593/K/1/3/37, Duke of Sutherland
to James Loch, 19 November 1849, Duchess
of Sutherland to James Loch, 22 November
1849, 23 November 1849.

63 SCRO, D593/K/1/3/47, Duchess of
Sutherland to George Loch, n.d. [(?)
October 1859].

64 Ibid., Thomas Higg to George Loch,
26 October 1859.

65 SCRO, D593/K/1/3/47, Duchess of
Sutherland to George Loch.

66 SCRO, D593/K/1/3/48, Duchess of
Sutherland to George Loch, 29 April 1860.

67 SCRO, D593/Q/1/6, John Fish to Thomas
Jackson, 31 January 1861.

68 Ibid., John Fish to Henry Wright, 24 July
1875.

69 NAL, 55C, diary of Sir Henry Cole
(typescript). 19 May 1878.

70 SCRO, D593/Q/2/1/2, John Fish to the Duke
of Sutherland, 7 June 1880.

71 SCRO, D593/Q/2/1/1, John Fish to Henry

[72] SCRO, D593/Q/2/1/2, John Fish to Henry Wright, 2nd April 1879.

[72] SCRO, D593/Q/2/1/2, John Fish to Henry Wright, 28 November 1882, 14 December 1882.

[73] SCRO, D593/Q/2/1/6, John Fish to the Duke of Sutherland, 12 August 1890.

[74] SCRO, D593/Q/1/7, G. Green, Electric Wiring & Fittings Co., Ltd to the Duke of Sutherland, 21 May 1891; London, PRO, Works 12/239, Chief Engineer's Report, n.d. (c. July 1913).

[75] SCRO, D593/K/1/9/45, John Culverwell to the Duke of Sutherland, 20 May 1897.

[76] SCRO, D593/K/1/9/34, Bedford Lemère to Alex Simpson, 5 March 1896.

[77] PRO, Works, 12/239, Chief Engineer's Report, n.d. (c. July 1913).

[78] CHRISTOPHER SIMON SYKES, *Private Palaces: Life in the Great London Houses*, London (Chatto & Windus) 1985, p. 258.

[79] *The Times*, 29 July 1856.

[80] *The Times*, 21 March 1853.

[81] *The Times*, 6 May 1864.

[82] H.G.C. MATTHEW (ed.), *The Gladstone Diaries*, 14 vols., Oxford (Oxford University Press) 1968–94, V, p. 386.

[83] DCMR, Lord Ronald Gower's diaries, 10 May 1859.

[84] *Ibid.*, 13 April 1864.

[85] SCRO, D593/P/25/1/2, William Ferguson to the Duke of Sutherland, 17 April 1864, 23 April 1864.

[86] DCMR, Lord Ronald Gower's diaries, 19 April 1864.

[87] Jasper Ridley, *Garibaldi*, London (Constable) 1974, p. 557.

[88] *Ibid.*, p. 558.

[89] DCMR, Lord Ronald Gower's diaries, 25 April, 1864.

[90] Richards 1973, p. 61.

[91] *The Times*, 1 February 1842.

[92] *The Times*, 27 June 1844.

[93] WCRA, Queen Victoria's journals, 16 June 1847.

[94] WCRA, Queen Victoria's journals, 15 May 1848.

[95] *Illustrated London News*, 20 May 1848.

[96] A. HEDLEY (trans. and ed.), *Selected Correspondence of Frederick Chopin*, London 1962, p. 332, quoted in Sykes 1985, pp. 266–67.

[97] SCRO, D593/Q/1/6, Eugène Lami to Thomas Jackson, n.d. (partly legible postmark: July 1848).

[98] WCRA, Queen Victoria's journals, January–August 1849, 13 June 1849.

[99] *Ibid.*, 15 March 1866.

[100] Gower 1902, pp. 71–72.

[101] SCRO, D593/P/28/2, Edward, Prince of Wales to the 3rd Duchess of Sutherland, n.d.

[102] *Ibid.*, Edward, Prince of Wales, to the 3rd Duchess of Sutherland, n.d.

[103] *The Times*, 16 November 1869.

[104] MATTHEW 1968–94, VIII, p. 492.

[105] SCRO, D593/R/5/6, meal book, July 1883 – January 1887, 17 July 1884.

[106] SCRO, D593/Q/2/1/8, Algernon Borthwick to Henry Wright, 29 September 1892.

[107] NAL, Henry Cole diaries (typescript), 6 January 1878.

[108] GEORGE EARLE BUCKLE, *The Life of Benjamin Disraeli, Earl of Beaconsfield*, 6 vols., London (John Murray) 1920, V, p. 430.

[109] SCRO, D593/P/26/4/4.

[110] *The Times*, 13 May 1874.

[111] BL, Addl. MS 44546, William Gladstone to the Duke of Sutherland, 12 October 1882.

[112] SCRO, D593/P/26/3/3.

[113] NAL, Sir Henry Cole's diary (typescript), 29 June 1875.

[114] *Ibid.*, 6 April 1877.

[115] See note 1.

[116] *Punch*, 3 July 1875, p. 284.

[117] EDITH, MARCHIONESS OF LONDONDERRY, *Retrospect*, London (Frederick Miller) 1938, p. 40.

[118] *Ibid.*, p. 72.

[119] DENIS STUART, *Dear Duchess: Millicent Duchess of Sutherland, 1867–1955*, London (Victor Gollancz) 1982, p. 61.

[120] OLIVER, VISCOUNT ESHER (ed.), *Journals and Letters of Reginald, Viscount Esher*, 4 vols., London (Nicholson & Watson) 1934–38, II, pp. 82–83.

[121] ARNOLD BENNET, *The Card*, London (Methuen) 1911, p. 9.

[122] WILLIAM ROTHENSTEIN, *Men and Memories: Recollections of William Rothenstein, 1900–1922*, London (Faber & Faber) 1932, p. 71.

[123] *The Times*, 17 June 1901.

[124] *The Times*, 27 June 1901.

[125] I am most grateful to William Rieder, Chairman of European Sculpture and Decorative Arts, The Metropolitan Museum of Art, New York, for making available to me photocopies of his typescripts.

[126] *The Times*, 11 June 1908.

[127] *The Times*, 27 June 1911.

[128] I am most grateful to John Charlton FSA for supplying me with this anecdote.

[129] DCMR, Lord Ronald Gower's diaries, July 1911.

[130] See note 122.

[131] Spoken recollections of Charles Janson, husband of Elizabeth, Countess of Sutherland.

[132] Stuart 1982, p. 59.

Chapter 4

[1] ANNA B. JAMESON, *Companion to the most celebrated private galleries of art in London*, London (Saunders & Otley) 1844, pp. 167, 171.

[2] GUSTAV WAAGEN, *Treasures of Art in Great Britain*, 4 vols., London (John Murray) 1854–57, I, pp. 35–37, p. 17.

[3] *Ibid.*, pp. 10, 341, 83, 289.

[4] SCRO, D593/P/34/1/1–2, Marquis of Stafford's bank accounts with Messrs Child, 1792–1839, 2 March 1802, 2 May 1806; D593/P/34/1/6–8, Marquis of Stafford's bank accounts with Drummonds, 1803–33.

[5] JORDANA POMEROY, 'The Orléans Collection: Its Impact on the British Art World', *Apollo*, CXLV, February 1997, pp. 26–31.

[6] CHA, J14/27/1, *Memorandum for an agreement … between The most Noble Francis Egerton, Duke of Bridgewater … By kind permission of the Howard family.*

[7] CHA, J14/27/15, *Acct of the Italian Orleans Pictures sold to the Public from 26th December 1798 to 18th April 1799.*

[8] CHA, J14/27/10, *Account of the remaining part of the Orleans Collection of Italian Pictures sold by Order of the Right Honorable Howard & c. & c.*

[9] JOHN BRITTON FSA, *Catalogue Raisonné of the Pictures belonging to the Most Honourable the Marquis of Stafford in the Gallery of Cleveland House …*, London (Longman, Hurst, Reese & Orme) 1808, p. iii.

[10] WILLIAM BISSELL POPE (ed.), *The Diary of Benjamin Robert Haydon*, 5 vols., Cambridge, MA (Harvard University Press) 1961–63, II, pp. 337–38.

[11] KENNETH GARLICK, ANGUS MACINTYRE and KATHRYN CAVE (eds.), *The Diary by Joseph Farington, R.A.*, 16 vols., New Haven and London (Yale University Press) 1978–1984, XI, pp. 3919–20.

[12] SCRO, D593/P/34/1/1, bank account of Earl Gower (later Marquis of Stafford) with Messrs Child, 1792–1802, 5 November 1801, 2 June 1802; D593/P/34/1/6, Marquis of Stafford's bank account with Drummonds, 1803–14, 31 May 1803.

[13] SCRO, D593/C/23/10 (6): *An Inventory of the Paintings, Marble busts, Library Books & Co at Stafford House St. James's … December 1833.*

[14] SRO, GD268/219/32, Marchioness of Stafford to James Loch, 23 June 1827.

[15] SCRO, D593/P/34/1/8, Marquis of Stafford's bank account with Drummond's, 1825–29.

[16] WILLIAM BUCHANAN, *Memoires of Painting with a chronological history of the Importation of Pictures by the Great Masters into England since the French Revolution*, 2 vols., London (Ackermann) 1824, II, pp. 178–79.

[17] SCRO, D593/R/2/19/32, John Henning's bill for 27 August 1840.

[18] WAAGEN 1854–57, I, p. 60.

[19] GARLICK et al. 1978–84, IV, p. 1511.

[20] See chapter 1, note 111.

[21] SCRO, D593/R/1/18/1, private secretary's account book (Jan 1845 – June 1855).

[22] LORD RONALD GOWER FSA, *Stafford House*, 2 vols., part of the series Great English Collections, Paris (Goupil) 1910.

[23] LORD RONALD GOWER FSA (ed.), *The Stafford House Letters*, London (Kegan Paul) 1891, p. 125.

[24] NLOS, Dep. 313/793, Antonio Canova to Earl Gower, 8 August 1818.

[25] SCRO, D593/R/2/17/15, 'Brown Scagliola Works, 20 June 1836'.

[26] SCRO, D593/Q/1/3, Bertel Thorvaldsen to Earl Gower, July 1829; NLOS, Dep. 313/802, Earl Gower's bank account, 15 August 1829.

[27] *The Art-Union*, VIII, 1846, pp. 237–39.

[28] SCRO, D593/P/22/1/5, Lord Francis Egerton to the Duke of Sutherland, 22 March 1834.

[29] NLOS, Dep. 313/830, Duke of Sutherland to the Duchess Countess of Sutherland, 8 April 1836; SCRO, D593/P/34/2/2, Duke of Sutherland's bank account, 1 December 1836.

[30] SCRO, D593/P/22/1/19, Benjamin Haydon to the Duke of Sutherland, 7 November 1837.

[31] Pope 1961–63, IV, p. 446–47.

[32] SCRO, D593/P/34/2/2, Duke of Sutherland's bank account, 6 April, 8 November 1836.

[33] NLOS, Dep. 313/830, Duke of Sutherland to the Duchess Countess of Sutherland, 25 March 1836.

[34] NLOS, Dep. 313/764, Duchess Countess of Sutherland to the 2nd Duke of Sutherland, 26 March 1836.

[35] NLOS, Dep. 313/830, Duke of Sutherland to the Duchess Countess of Sutherland, 19 March 1836.

[36] SCRO, D593/Q/1/3, S. Gunn, n.d. (the rate of exchange at the time (see Vantini's cash book, D593/R/1/14/1) was at that time 25.50 francs to £1).

[37] SCRO, D593/Q/1/3, Lesage, November 1835.

[38] SCRO, D593/R/2/21/5, Chasses, Tapissier, 17 April 1840.

[39] Gower 1891, p. 217.

[40] SCRO, D593/R/2/21/1, 'Note des Objets achetés & commandés par l'Entremise de Ant. Lynen', n.d. (c. November 1837).

[41] Philip Ward-Jackson: 'A.-E. Carrier-Belleuse, J.-J. Feuchère and the Sutherlands', *Burlington Magazine*, CXXVII, no. 948, March 1985, pp. 146–53.

[42] SCRO, D593/Q/1/3, Antoine Lynen, 2 June 1838.

[43] Gower 1891, pp. 215–16.

[44] SCRO, D593/R/7/15, Stafford House inventory, 1839, p. 85; *Art-Union*, 1847, pp.

[45] SCRO, D593/R/7/14, Alexandre Lenoir to Dominic Colnaghi, 27 November 1837; bill of Paul & Dominic Colnaghi, 30 November 1837 – 3 May, 1838.

[46] DCRM, Lord Ronald Gower's diaries, 29 June 1874.

[47] SCRO, D593/R/7/15, Stafford House inventory, 1839, p. 77.

[48] SCRO, D593/K/1/3/32, P. Frazer Tyler to James Loch, n.d. (c. September 1844).

[49] Gower 1883, II, p. 69.

[50] *The Times*, 2 December 1874.

[51] SCRO, D593/Q/1/3, Thomas Jackson to Carlo Galvani, 2 September 1841.

[52] SCRO, D593/Q/2/1/1, Thomas Jackson to Henry Wright, 9 April 1864.

[53] Gower 1910, I, no. 1.

[54] SCRO, D593/Q/1/3, Thomas Jackson to Signor Galvani, 2 September 1841.

[55] London, The National Gallery: *Catalogue of the Gallery of His Royal Highness the Duke of Lucca, now exhibiting at the Gallery of the Society of Painters in Water-Colours … July, 1840*: lot 3. Gerardo della Notte: *Christ before Caiaphas* … lot 68. L. Penni: *Virgin and Child* [unfortunately, this catalogue is not priced]; Stowe 1854, pp. 215–16.

[56] LYTTON STRACHEY and ROGER FULFORD (eds.), *The Greville Memoirs, 1814–1856*, 8 vols., London (Macmillan) 1938, III, p. 255.

[57] SCRO, D593/R/2/42/2, Tatam & Mudie to Thomas Jackson, 17 January 1846: "112 Naps @ £23-10-0 £2,632".

[58] SCRO, D593/P/22/4/4, Giuseppe Gallo Lorenzi to the Duchess of Sutherland, 7 December 1841.

[59] SCRO, D593/P/22/1/28, Giuseppe Gallo Lorenzi to the Duchess of Sutherland, 21 July 1845.

[60] SCRO, D593/P/22/4/4, Holme & Co. to Thomas Jackson, 3 June 1843.

[61] See note 59.

[62] SCRO, D593/P/22/1/28, Giuseppe Gallo Lorenzi to Thomas Jackson, 8 September 1846.

[63] *Ibid.*, Giuseppe Gallo Lorenzi to the Duchess of Sutherland, 26 May 1845.

[64] *Ibid.*, Giuseppe Gallo Lorenzi to the Duchess of Sutherland, 21 July 1845.

[65] SCRO, D593/Q/1/3, Giuseppe Gallo Lorenzi to the Duchess of Sutherland, 31 December 1847.

[66] SCRO, D593/R/31/1, George Morant & Son, 6 March 1847, 23 June 1847.

[67] SCRO, D593/P/22/1/18, Sir Thomas Lawrence to Earl Gower, 27 December 1824, 5 July 1828.

[68] Gower 1910, I, no. 3.

[69] Stowe 1854, p. 211.

[70] See note 68.

[71] WCRA, Queen Victoria's journals, 13 June 1849.

[72] SCRO, D593/P/34/2/4, Duke of Sutherland's bank account, 7 July 1852.

[73] Sotheby's, 5 November 1969, lot 107 (south section); Christie's, 2 July 1971, lot 113, (central section); Sotheby's, Chester, 29 April 1990, lot 3193 (central section), withdrawn; Sotheby's, London, 11 July 1990, lot 113.

[74] Christie's, 15 December 1972, lot 86.

[75] Gower 1902, p. 63.

[76] See note 71.

[77] I am most grateful to Clare Bunkham, The National Gallery, London, for her information.

[78] SCRO, D593/R/2/42/3, Edward Price to Thomas Jackson, 27 December 1848; D593/R/2/42/2, Mrs Scriven to the Duke of Sutherland, 27 March 1846.

[79] SCRO, D593/Q/1/1/3, John Francis to the Duke of Sutherland, 1 May 1854.

[80] Pope 1961–63, V, p. 347.

[81] *Ibid.*, IV, p. 247; SCRO, D593/P/22/1/17, Benjamin Haydon to the Duke of

Sutherland, December 1834.
82 SCRO, D593/P/22/1/19.
83 The priced sale catalogue in the Christie's Archive remains untraced.
84 SCRO, D593/R/1/18/1, Duke of Sutherland's account book, Jan 1845 – June 1855.
85 SCRO, D593/P/22/1/28, Duke of Sutherland to Lord Stafford, 13 May 1848, John G. Lough to the Duke of Sutherland, 20 May 1848; D593/R/7/19, Stafford House inventory, 1857, p. 101.
86 SCRO, D593/R/2/42/3, George Morant & Son, 3 January – 29 April 1847.
87 SCRO, D593/P/22/4/4, George Morant to Thomas Jackson, 23 March 1846.
88 SCRO, D593/K/1/5/55, James Loch to the Duchess of Sutherland, 21 April 1848.
89 SCRO, D593/R/2/42/1, M. Crozatier, n.d., c. early 1848.
90 SCRO, D593/K/1/3/43, Duke of Sutherland to James Loch, 1 October 1855.
91 SCRO, D593/P/22/1/28, Herbert Minton, 13 February 1858.
92 SCRO, D593/Q/1/3, London, Emmanuel Brothers, 16 March 1835.
93 The Times, 1 February 1842.
94 SCRO, D593/R/1/10a, 'Mr Lilly's accounts ... 27th August 1790 – 10th November 1792'.
95 JAMES LOCH, Memoir of George Granville, late Duke of Sutherland, K.G., London 1834, p. 19.
96 SCRO, D593/R/2/19/19, E.H. Baldock, June 1839.
97 SCRO, D593/R/2/16/15: E.H. Baldock, 13 February – 17 September 1835.
98 SCRO, D593/K/1/3/34, Duke of Sutherland to James Loch, 26 December 1846.
99 SCRO, D593/C/23/10(6), An Inventory of the Paintings ... December 1833.
100 SCRO, D593/R/2/21/3.
101 SCRO, D593/R/7/17.
102 SCRO, D593/Q/1/3, Antoine Lynen, 27 June 1838.
103 SCRO, D593/Q/1/3, George Gropius, 15 June 1838.
104 SCRO, D593/Q/1/3. The sofa cost 1,225 Prussian thalers. The sculptor was August Kleemeyer, the joiner J.W. Bidtel and the upholsterer A. Schild.
105 SCRO, D593/P/22/1/28, John Martin to the Duchess of Sutherland, September 1839.
106 SCRO, D593/Q/1/1/1, Duchess of Sutherland to Thomas Jackson, n.d.; D593/R/2/42/1, Abraham Kent, 2–23 March 1846.
107 SCRO, D593/K/1/3/40, Duke of Sutherland to James Loch, 28 May 1852.
108 The Times, 1 February 1842.
109 SCRO, D593/P/22/1/3, Lord Brougham to the Duke of Sutherland, n.d.
110 SCRO, D593/K/1/3/33, n.d. [among letters for April 1845].
111 SCRO, D593/K/1/3/36, Duchess of Sutherland to James Loch, 4 April 1848.
112 SCRO, D593/K/1/3/39, Thomas Jackson to James Loch, 4 June 1851.
113 Gower 1902, p. 57.
114 DCMR, Lord Ronald Gower's diaries, 3 July 1887.
115 NAL, 55C, Sir Henry Cole's diary, 23 August 1838.
116 W.M. ROSSETTI (ed.), Ruskin: Rossetti: Preraphaelitism – Papers – Papers 1854 to 1862, London (Allen) 1899, pp. 40–41. I am most grateful to the late Dr Clive Wainwright FSA for referring me to this source.
117 SCRO, D593/Q/2/1/1, Thomas Jackson to Henry Wright, 1 January 1863.
118 SCRO, D593/Q/3/14.
119 The Times, 2 May 1862.
120 The Times, 30 June 1876.
121 SCRO, D593/Q/2/1/1, S. Birch to Henry Wright, 14 June 1875, Richard Owen to

Henry Wright, 2 July 1875; NAL, Sir Henry Cole's diary, 15 July 1875.
122 SCRO, D593/Q/2/1/1, S. Birch to Henry Wright, 23 July 1875.
123 SCRO, D593/P/24/1/4 William Blundell Spence to the 3rd Duke of Sutherland, 30 November 1888 (although this is a letter of condolence, Spence wrote in fairly familiar tones).
124 SCRO, D593/K/1/3/50, Dowager Duchess of Sutherland to George Loch, 11 December 1862; D593/R/2/84, Matthew Noble, 9 April 1875; Matthew 1968–94, VII, p. 304.
125 DCMR, Stafford House inventory, 1896, p. 67.
126 SCRO, D593/R/2/84, receipt for £300 signed by Odoardo Fantacchiotti, 21 January 1867.
127 NAL, Sir Henry Cole's diary, 23 April 1875, 24 July 1875.
128 DCMR, Stafford House inventory, 1896.
129 SCRO, D593/Q/2/1/1 Richard Smart to Henry Wright, 9 September 1879.
130 SCRO, D593/1/K/5/137, George Loch to W. Woodall, 17 June 1865.
131 SCRO, D593/Q/2/1/7, J. Comyns Carr to the Duke of Sutherland, 9 October 1891.
132 SCRO, D593/K/1/7/5, George Loch to the Duke of Sutherland, 23 January 1877; Eric Richards, 'An Anatomy of the Sutherland Fortune: Income, Consumption, Investments and Returns, 1780–1880', Business History, XXI, no. 1, 1979, pp. 45–78.
133 Gower 1883, p. 68.
134 ROTHS. 00/174, E. Joseph to Alfred de Rothschild, 3 November 1876.
135 SCRO, D593/R/7/15, Stafford House inventory, 1839, p. 46.
136 Gower 1910, II, no. 5.
137 STUART 1982, pp. 35–36.
138 The Times, 10 February 1908.
139 CA, annotated copy of Catalogue of important pictures by Old Masters. Works of the Early English School and Modern Pictures ... removed from Stafford House ... Trentham Hall ... Lilleshall House, 8 February 1908.
140 GABRIEL MOUREY, 'La Collection du duc de Sutherland à Stafford House', Les Arts, no. 133, 1913, pp. 2–32.
141 CA, Catalogue of Ancient and Modern Pictures, the property of the Duke of Sutherland, K.G., removed from Stafford House ..., 11 July 1913 (priced catalogue).
142 SCRO, D593/R/2/15/16, Charles Smith, 15 October 1835.
143 NAL, Hanover Square rooms priced catalogue, Catalogue of the Remaining Portion of the Stafford House Furniture etc. to be sold at Auction by Messrs Knight, Frank & Rutley, 14th, 15th 25th July 1913 (only the sales for the first day are priced).
144 PRO, Works, 12/239, A Schedule of Items agreed to be purchased by Sir Wm Lever for the sum of £1,750, n.d. ([?] July 1913); Stafford House – Articles probably purchased by Sir William Lever, 25 April 1923; List of furniture purchased with Treasury Grant at sale of Lancaster House furniture, July 1913.
145 BL, British Library Catalogues, no. 1199, Sotheby, Wilkinson & Hodge, 15 October – 3 November 1913.

Chapter 5

1 PRO, Crest 35/2429, George Leveson-Gower to the 4th Duke of Sutherland, 10 July 1911.
2 Stuart 1982, p. 118.
3 SCRO, D593/P/22/1/2, Lord Melbourne to the Duke of Sutherland, 19 January 1841; Lord Melbourne to the Duchess of Sutherland, 28 January 1841.
4 DAVID CANNADINE, The Decline and Fall of

the British Aristocracy, New Haven CT and London (Yale University Press) 1990, pp. 48–50.
5 GILES ST AUBYN, Edward VII: Prince and King, London (Collins) 1979, p. 154.
6 SCRO, D593/K/1/3/55, Duke of Sutherland to George Loch, 5 August 1867.
7 SCRO, D593/K/1/5/166, George Loch to the Duchess of Sutherland, 7 July 1872.
8 THE DUKE OF SUTHERLAND, Looking Back, London (Oldham Press) 1957, p. 38.
9 SCRO, D593/P/30/1, Henry Wright to Lord Stafford, 1 May 1889.
10 DCMR, Lord Ronald Gower's diaries, 26 November 1888.
11 SCRO, D593/R/5/5, meal book, July 1881 – June 1883.
12 SCRO, D593/K/1/7/47, Henry Wright to Edward Humbert, 5 June 1894.
13 SCRO, D593/P/24/1/4.
14 DCRO, D/LO/F631 (1), Copy – Pamphlet printed and issued by the Duchess Dowager of Sutherland, June 1892. Observations by Lord Stafford, Trentham (privately printed) 1892, p. 3.
15 Ibid., p. 3.
16 DCRO, D/LO/F631 (70), Sutherland & others v. Sutherland – Further observations & summary of evidence, March 1894, p. 3.
17 SCRO, D593/P/29/1/22.
18 DCRO, D/LO/F631(32), Duchess Mary Caroline to Marquis of Stafford, 10 August 1890; Marquis of Stafford to Duchess Mary Caroline, 30 August 1890.
19 DCMR, Lord Ronald Gower's diaries, 26 November 1888.
20 See note 14, op. cit., p. 4.
21 DCRO, D/LO/F631(21), Marquis of Stafford to Henry Chaplin, 15 November 1891.
22 DCRO, D/LO/F631(41), R.S. Taylor to Henry Chaplin, 1 July 1892.
23 DCRO, D/LO/F631(42), R.S. Taylor to the Marquis of Stafford, 25 August 1892.
24 DCMR, Lord Ronald Gower's diaries, 28 September 1892.
25 DCRO, D/LO/F631(21), 4th Duke of Sutherland to Henry Chaplin, 1 October 1892.
26 DCMR, Lord Ronald Gower's diaries, 21 October 1892.
27 DCRO, D/LO/F631(44), Richard Taylor to Henry Wright, 1 October 1892.
28 DCRO, D/LO/F631(43), Richard Taylor to Henry Wright, 30 September 1892.
29 The Times, 19 April 1893.
30 The Times, 29 April 1893, H.H. Asquith's reply to questions from Mr Warmington, Mr A. Morton and Mr Lough.
31 The Times, 28 April 1893.
32 SCRO, D593/K/1/9/43, John Culverwell to Richard Taylor, 3 August 1892; John Culverwell to the Duke of Sutherland, 4 August 1894. (In the index at the beginning of this letter book Culverwell wrote: "Stocks to be sold to realize £500,000 for Dowager.")
33 SCRO, D593/K/1/7/47, Henry Wright to E. Humbert, 8 June 1894.
34 DCRO, D/LO/F631(21), Lord Stafford to Henry Chaplin, 15 November 1891.
35 SCRO, D593/K/1/5/84, George Loch to the Duchess of Sutherland, 25 July 1855.
36 SCRO, D593/P/30/1, Duke of Sutherland to Mr Homer, 20 October 1905.
37 The Times, 24 July 1906.
38 PR, f. 1469, p. 2, 'The last will of Cromartie Duke and Earl of Sutherland K.G. made 28 January 1913'.
39 EP, Esher, 2/12.
40 PRO, Crest 35/2429, The Rt Hon. Sir William Carrington to George Leveson-Gower, 21 August 1911.
41 Ibid., George Leveson-Gower to Sir William

Carrington, 1911.
42 The Times, 13 November 1912.
43 DCMR, Lord Ronald Gower's diaries, 7 November 1912.
44 The Times, 1 January 1913.
45 The Times, 29 March 1913.
46 The Times, 3 May 1913.
47 PRO, Works 12/239, memoranda; W.H. Leverhulme, 2nd Viscount Leverhulme, Viscount Leverhulme by his Son, London (Allen & Unwin) 1927, p. 253.
48 DCMR, Lord Ronald Gower's diaries, 8 November 1912.
49 THE MARCHIONESS OF LONDONDERRY, Henry Chaplin, a Memoir, London (Macmillan) 1926, p. 144.
50 Stuart 1982, p. 188.
51 Francis Sheppard, The Treasury of London's Past, London (HMSO) 1991.
52 PRO, T1/11564/17176, Sir Lewis Harcourt MP to Sir R. Chalmers, 5 May 1913.
53 SIR MORTIMER WHEELER, Still Digging, London (Michael Joseph) 1955, p. 85.
54 Ibid., p. 84.
55 Ibid., p. 107.
56 I am most grateful to Ken Clare for allowing me to see (unindexed) scrapbooks and menu plans at the Foreign and Commonwealth Office Archives, Hanslope Park, nr Milton Keynes.
57 PRO, Work 12/441, no. 42, Ernest Bevin to George Tomlinson, 10 August 1945.
58 Ibid., no. 46, Ernest Bevin to George Tomlinson, 23 August 1945.
59 Ibid., no. 59, 1 October 1946.
60 PRO, Work 12/899, 'Note of a Meeting held at Lambeth Bridge House on 15 July 1952'.
61 Ibid., General C.D. Steel to R.T. Beaumont, 29 November 1952, 3 December 1952.
62 See note 60.
63 Ibid., F.J. Root, Lancaster House, 15 May 1952.
64 The Times, 14 July 1953.
65 Evening Standard, 28 August 1953.
66 Evening News, 1 September 1953.
67 CHRISTOPHER HUSSEY, 'Restoration of Lancaster House', Country Life, CXIV, no. 2965, 12 November 1953, p. 1576.
68 PRO, Work 12/444, no. 186, The Rt Hon. Alan Lennox-Boyd MP to the Rt Hon. Patrick Buchan-Hepburn MP, 4 February 1956.
69 The Times, 16 March 1961.
70 Lord Carrington, Reflect on Things Past, London (Collins) 1988, p. 290.

Conclusion

1 Gower 1883, pp. 6–7.
2 Matthew 1968–94, III, p. 9.
3 F.H.W. SHEPHERD (ed.), Survey of London, XL: The Grosvenor Estate in Mayfair, part II, 'The Buildings', London (Athlone Press) 1980, pp. 247–48.
4 The Builder, LXXI, no. 2801, 10 October 1896, p. 290.
5 Crook 1999, p. 183.
6 The Times, 28 June 1849, p. 8.
7 Sykes 1985, p. 301.
8 SCRO, D593/K/1/3/32, untitled schedule included with letters for April 1844.
9 Hussey 1953, pp. 1572–76.

Select Bibliography

SAMUEL and SARAH ADAMS, The Complete Servant, London (Knight and Lacey) 1825
WINSLOW AMES, 'The Completion of Stafford House', in Douglas Fraser, Howard Hibbard and Milton Lewine (eds.), Essays in the History of Architecture Presented to Rudolf Wittkower, 2 vols., London (Phaidon) 1967, I,

pp. 217–18

Francis Bamford and the Duke of Wellington (eds.), *The Journal of Mrs Arbuthnot, 1820–1832*, 2 vols., London (Macmillan) 1950

David Blisset, 'Sir Charles Barry (1795–1860): A Reassessment of his Travels and Early Career', unpublished doctoral dissertation, Oxford Polytechnic, November 1982

Jacques-François Blondel, *De la distribution des maisons de plaisance*, Paris 1737

Germain Boffrand, *Livre d'architecture*, Paris 1745

John Britton fsa, *Catalogue Raisonné of the Pictures belonging to the Most Honourable the Marquis of Stafford in the Gallery of Cleveland House …*, London (Longman, Hurst, Rees & Orme) 1808

W. Buchanan, *Memoires of Painting with a chronological history of the Importation of Pictures by the Great Masters into England since the French Revolution*, 2 vols., London (Ackermann) 1824

David Cannadine, *The Decline and Fall of the British Aristocracy*, New Haven ct and London (Yale University Press) 1990

E. Beresford Chancellor, *The Private Palaces of London*, London (Kegan Paul) 1908

Christie, Manson & Woods, *Important Pictures by Old Masters/Works of the Early English School and Modern Pictures, the Property of His Grace the Duke of Sutherland, k.g., removed from Stafford House …, Trentham Hall …, and Lilleshall House …*, 5 February 1908

——, *Ancient and Modern Pictures of the late Duke of Sutherland k.g. removed from Stafford House …*, 11 July 1913

A.F. Circket, 'History of Wrest House', *Bedfordshire Historical Record Society*, lix, 1980, pp. 65–87

Frances Collard, *Regency Furniture*, Woodbridge, Suffolk (Antique Collector's Club) 1985

H.M. Colvin, 'The Architects of Stafford House', *Architectural History*, 1, 1958, pp. 17–30

John Cornforth, 'Trentham, Staffordshire – formerly a seat of the Dukes of Sutherland', *Country Life*, cxliii, no. 3699, 25 January 1968, no. 3700, 1 February 1968, pp. 176–80, 228–31

——, 'Stafford House Revisited' – parts I and II, *Country Life*, cxlv, no. 3740, 7 November 1968, no. 3741, 14 November 1968, pp. 1188–91, 1257–61

James Crathorne, *Cliveden: The Place and the People*, London (Collins & Brown) 1995

J. Mordant Crook, *The Rise of the Nouveaux Riches*, London (John Murray) 1999

Geoffrey de Bellaigue and Pat Kirkham, 'George IV and the Furnishing of Windsor Castle', *Furniture History*, viii, 1972, pp. 1–34

Revd Irwin Eller, *The History of Belvoir Castle from the Norman Conquest to the Nineteenth Century*, London (R. Tyas) 1841

Joseph Friedman, *Spencer House: Chronicle of a Great London Mansion*, London (Zwemmer) 1993

Frederick Augustus, Duke of York and Albany (Anon.), *The Debts of His Royal Highness the Duke of York. Extracts from the London Daily and Weekly Press*, London 1831

Roger Fulford, *Royal Dukes: The Father and Uncles of Queen Victoria* [1933], London (Collins) 1973

Kenneth Garlick, *Sir Thomas Lawrence: A Complete Catalogue of the Oil Paintings*, Oxford (Phaidon) 1989

Kenneth Garlick, Angus Macintyre and Kathryn Cave (eds.), *The Diary by Joseph*

Farington, r.a., 16 vols., New Haven and London (Yale University Press) 1978–84

Lord Ronald Gower fsa, *The Lenoir collection of original French prints at Stafford House*, London (Maclure & Macdonald) 1874

——, *My Reminiscences*, 2 vols., London (Kegan Paul) 1883

——, *The Stafford House Letters*, London (Kegan Paul) 1891

——, *Stafford House*, part of the series Great English Collections, Paris (Goupil) 1910

Lytton Strachey and Roger Fulford (eds.), *The Greville Memoirs, 1814–1856*, 8 vols., London (Macmillan) 1938

Michael Hall, 'Ducal Designs', *Country Life*, cxc, no. 11, 14 March 1996, pp. 34–37

John Hardy, 'The Building and Decoration of Apsley House', *Apollo*, xcviii, no. 139, September 1973, pp. 12–21

John Harris, 'C.R. Cockerell's "Ichnographica Domestica"', *Architectural History*, xiv, 1971

W. Hazlitt, *Criticism in Art* (reprint), to which is attached *Catalogue of the Pictures of Stafford House*, London (Templeman) 1844

Simon Houffe, 'Wrest Park, Bedfordshire', – parts I and II, *Country Life*, cxliii, 25 June 1970, pp. 1250–53, cxlviii, 2 July 1970, pp. 18–21

Christopher Hussey, 'Restoration of Lancaster House', *Country Life*, cxiv, 12 November 1953, pp. 1572–76

——, 'Belvoir Castle, Leicestershire' – parts I, II, III, IV, *Country Life*, cxx, 6 December 1956, 13 December 1956, 20 December 1956, 27 December 1956, pp. 1284–90, 1402–05, 1456–59, 1500–03

——, *English Country Houses: Late Georgian, 1800–1840*, London (Country Life) 1958

Philip Ward Jackson, 'A.-E. Carrier Belleuse, J.-J. Feuchère and the Sutherlands', *Burlington Magazine*, cxxvii, no. 984, March 1985, pp. 146–53

Anna B. Jameson, *Companion to the most celebrated private galleries of art in London*, London (Saunders & Otley) 1844

Simon Jervis, 'The Rococo Revival', in Simon Jervis, *High Victorian Design*, Woodbridge (Suffolk Boydell) 1983, pp. 37–58

Edward Joy, *English Furniture, 1800–1850*, London (Sotheby's, Parke Bernet) 1977

C.M. Matthew, *Catalogue of Paintings in the Wellington Museum*, London (HMSO) 1982

Fiske Kimball, *The Creation of the Rococo Style*, Philadelphia (Philadelphia Museum of Art) 1943; edn used New York (Dover) 1980

Knight, Frank & Rutley, *Catalogue of the Remaining Portion of the Stafford House Furniture to be sold at Auction …*, 14, 15, 25 July 1913

Tim Knox, 'Losing Thorvaldsen's Leveson-Gower: The Rediscovery of Earl Gower's Bust at Cliveden', *Apollo*, cxliii, no. 410, April 1996, pp. 37–43

Maude, Lady Leconfield (ed.), revised and completed by John Gore, *The Three Howard Sisters*, London (Murray) 1955

James Loch, *Memoir of George Granville, late Duke of Sutherland*, London 1834

Jean Mariette, *L'Architecture françoise*, 4 vols., Paris 1727–38

H.G.C. Matthew (ed.), *The Gladstone Diaries*, 14 vols., Oxford (Oxford University Press) 1968–94

Gabriel Mourey, 'La Collection du duc de Sutherland à Stafford House', *Les Arts*, no. 133, 1913, pp. 2–32

M. Passavant, *Tour of a German Artist in England*, 2 vols., London (Saunders & Otley) 1836

David Pearce, *London's Mansions: The Palatial Houses of the Nobility*, London (Batsford) 1986

Jordana Pomeroy, 'The Orléans Collection: Its Impact on the British Art World', *Apollo*, cxlv, no. 420, February 1997, pp. 26–31

William Bissell Pope (ed.), *The Diary of Benjamin Robert Haydon*, 5 vols., Cambridge ma (Harvard University Press) 1961–63

Eric Richards, *The Leviathan of Wealth*, London (Routledge & Kegan Paul) 1973

——, *A History of the Highland Clearances*, London (Croom Helm) 1982–85

——, 'An Anatomy of the Sutherland Fortune: Income, Consumption, Investments and Returns, 1780–1880', *Business History*, xxi, no. 1, 1979, pp. 45–78

Jasper Ridley, *Garibaldi*, London (Constable) 1974

John Martin Robinson, *The Wyatts: An Architectural Dynasty*, intro. by Woodrow Wyatt, Oxford (Oxford University Press) 1974

John Martin Robinson, 'Sir Frederick Trench and London Improvements', *History Today*, xxvii, no. 5, May 1977, pp. 324–31

Elizabeth, Duchess of Rutland, *Journal of a Trip to Paris by the Duke and Duchess of Rutland, July MDCCCXIV*, London 1815

Francis Sheppard, *The Treasury of London's Past*, London (HMSO) 1991

Sotheby, Wilkinson & Hodge, *Catalogue of a portion of the Library of Stafford House, St. James's s.w., sold under the instructions of his Grace the Duke of Sutherland …*, 29, 30, 31 October 1913

R. Stanley-Morgan, 'Benjamin Wyatt and his Noble Clients', *Architectural Review*, cxlv, February 1969

Harriet Beecher Stowe, *Sunny Memories of Foreign Lands*, London (Sampson, Lowe & Co) 1854

Denis Stuart, *Dear Duchess: Millicent Duchess of Sutherland, 1867–1955*, London (Gollancz) 1982

George Granville Sutherland Sutherland-Leveson-Gower, Duke of Sutherland, *The Story of Stafford House*, London (Geoffrey Bless) 1935

——, *Looking Back*, London (Oldham Press) 1957

Mary Caroline, Dowager Duchess of Sutherland, *Pamphlet printed and issued by the Duchess Dowager of Sutherland, June 1892*, Trentham 1892

Christopher Simon Sykes, *Private Palaces: Life in the Great London Houses*, London (Chatto & Windus) 1985

F.M.L. Thompson, *English Landed Society in the 19th Century*, London (Routledge & Kegan Paul) 1963

Sir Frederick William Trench, *Thames Quay, with Hints for some further improvements in the metropolis*, London (Carpenter) 1827

Gustav Waagen, *Treasures of Art in Great Britain*, 4 vols., London (John Murray) 1854–57

R.F. Wisker, 'The Dukes of Sutherland and Staffordshire in the Early Nineteenth Century', unpublished ma diss., University of Birmingham, October 1974

James Yorke, 'Better than any original' [the scagliola of William Croggon], *Country Life*, clxxxvii, 1 April 1993, pp. 54–55

——, 'Belvoir Castle, Leicestershire' – parts I and II, *Country Life*, clxxxviii, 23 June 1994, 30 June 1994, pp. 89–93, 62–65

——, 'The Furnishing of Stafford House by Nicholas Morel, 1828–1830', *Furniture History*, xxxii, 1996, pp. 46–80

——, 'Desiré Dellier – "Arrant Scoundrel"', *Furniture History*, xxxii, 1997, pp. 259–63

——, 'The History of Stafford House, 1825–1913', unpublished doctoral dissertation, University of London, May 1998

——, 'The Work of John Henning Jr. at Stafford

House', *Apollo*, cxlix, no. 443, January 1999, pp. 43–48

Picture Credits

Grateful acknowledgements are owed to the following for supplying photographic material and for permission to reproduce it:

pl. 84 © Ackerman and Johnson Ltd, London/Bridgeman Art Library, London

pls. 78, 81 © Algur H. Meadows Collection, Southern Methodist University, Dallas

pl. 36 © Ashmolean Museum of Art and Archaeology, Oxford

pls. 40, 43, 47, 58 © Bibliothèque Nationale, Paris

pl. 6 © British Museum, London

pls. 5, 19, 34 © Country Life

pls. 11, 37, © 2000 Her Majesty Queen Elizabeth II

illus. pages 6–7, frontispiece, pls. 1, 2, 15, 20, 24, 30, 32, 52, 56, 59, 62, 64, 67, 76, 98, 99, 103, 104, 106, 108 © Mark Fiennes

pl. 105 © Foreign and Commonwealth Office, London

pls. 21, 83 © Government Collection of Works of Art, London

pl. 33 © London Metropolitan Archives

pls. 82, 91 © Norman Mays

pl. 86 © Minneapolis Institute of Art

pl. 79 © Museum Boymans–van Benningen, Rotterdam

pls. 13, 28, 97 © Museum of London

pl. 90 © The National Gallery, London

pls. 85, 89 © National Gallery of Art, Washington, DC

pl. 88 © National Gallery of Canada, Ottawa

pls. 22, 23, 29, 39, 46, 68, 69, 96 © National Monuments Record Office, London

pls. 3, 4, 7, 8, 14, 25, 65, 66, 102 © National Portrait Gallery, London

pl. 107 © Press Association, London

pl. 80 © Reunion des musées nationaux, France (photograph by D. Arnaudet and G. Blot)

pl. 41 © Réunion des musées nationaux, France (photograph by G. Blot)

pl. 42 © Réunion des musées nationaux, France (photograph by J. Derenne)

pl. 49 © Réunion des musées nationaux, France (photograph by H. Lewandowski)

pls. 10, 26, 27 © Royal Institute of British Architects, London

pls. 16, 92, 93, 94, 95 © Sutherland Trust, Dunrobin Castle, Sutherland (photographs by Sir Geoffrey Shakerley)

pls. 63, 70, 72, 73, 74, 75, 87, 101 © Sutherland Trust, Dunrobin Castle, Sutherland (photographs by David Sym)

pls. 12, 17, 18, 38, 44, 45, 48, 50, 51, 53, 54, 55, 57, 60, 61, 71, 77, 100 © Victoria and Albert Museum Picture Library, London

pl. 9 © Victoria and Albert Museum Picture Library, London (courtesy of Westminster City Archives, London)

pl. 35 courtesy of the Worshipful Company of Goldsmiths, London

pl. 31 © James Yorke

Index